D0952906

Design Language

"*The beginning of wisdom is to call things by their right names.*"

— *Chinese Proverb*

Design Language

Tim McCreight

Brynmorgen
Press

©1996
Brynmorgen Press, Inc.
33 Woodland Road
Cape Elizabeth, Maine 04107
207 767 6059   USA

Library of Congress Catalog Number:
ISBN: 0-9615984-6-8

Printed in China

10 9 8 7 6 5 4 3 2 1

Introduction

Design is essentially a private, idiosyncratic affair. Any attempt to write about design must understand that information is never truly meaningful until it has been creatively put to use. But we work in a world of interaction—between teachers and students, between artists and clients, and with our fellow designers. We need to communicate, and in some contexts our ideas are only as good as our ability to share them with others.

In the following pages you'll find reflections on the principles of design as revealed through conventional terminology. The alphabetical listing of 100 keywords provides a familiar, non-hierarchical organization that allows you to move into and around the book. Passages are brief and subjective, using dictionary extracts, etymology and a quotation from literature as tangent points. Each entry includes a list of associated keywords that encourage you to navigate from one idea to the next. This is not a picture book, but you should use it in conjunction with lots of picture books. And trips to the beach, the woods and the circus.

Design Language is a tool made of paper. Like other tools, it will function best when it's been modified to suit your needs, so make notes in the margins, add to the lists, and bend a few pages.

keywords

Abstract
Aesthetics
Anthropomorphic
Anticipation

Balance   -------
Beauty   -------
Boundary

Center
Closure
Collaboration
Collage
Composition
Compression
Concrete
Confidence
Content
Context
Continuity
Contour
Control
Contrast
Craft
Critique

Decorative
Density
Design
Dialogue
Dissonance
Dominance
Dynamic

Eclectic
Economy
Edge
Elegance
Emphasis
Entropy   -------
Ergonomics

Figure/Ground
Formal   -------
Fragment
Function   -------

Gestalt   -------
Gesture
Grid   -------
Grouping   -------

Harmony
Hierarchy   -------
Hue   -------

Icon
Innovation
Intersection
Integration
Integrity
Interval
Intuition
Invention

Ratio
Resolution
Rhythm

Join

Line
Linear

Scale
Sensuous/Sensual
Sentiment
Shape
Size
Space

Mass
Module
Monumentality
Motion

Structure
Stylization
Surreal
Symbol
Symmetry
Synesthesia

Negative/Positive

Template
Tension
Texture
Time

Order
Organic
Originality
Ornamental

Transformation
Transition

Parameters
Pattern
Perspective
Plane
Positive/Negative
Progression
Proximity

Unity

Value
Volume

Weight

Abstract

abstract (AB-strakt)

1 Considered apart from concrete existence

2 Not applied or practical; theoretical

3 Impersonal, as in attitude or views

4 Having an intellectual and affective artistic content that depends solely on intrinsic form rather than on narrative content or pictorial representation

5 To take away; remove

6 To summarize; epitomize. The concentrated essence of a larger whole

abstractus (Latin) = removed from (concrete reality)

Some people think abstract art means something weird looking; this is incorrect. Weird is easy, but abstract work springs from and must be responsive to, a physical reality.

A brief summary of a written treatise such as a dissertation is called an abstract. It is based on the real thing but is a more concise version, getting immediately at its essential character.

A dominant theme of all forms of art in the twentieth century is alienation. Humankind is seen as removed from Nature, out of touch with inner or animal needs, disconnected from social bonds and lacking a sense of continuity in time. Given all this, is it any wonder that abstract art is a central response?

Abstract art comes from spirit rather than from nature and in this sense abstract art is spiritual and uniquely human. Because abstraction is rooted in humanness as distinct from "American-ness" or "male-ness," it complements the world unity found in technology and science. A color field painting, for instance, can speak outside the restrictions of language, culture and geography.

SEE:

Content
Distort
Fragment
Transformation

"*There is no abstract art.
You must always start with something.*"

– Pablo Picasso

"Written truth is four-dimensional. If we consult it at the wrong time, or read it at the wrong pace, it is as empty and shapeless as a dress on a hook"

— Robert Grudin

Aesthetics

Aesthetics (asz THET iks)

1 **The criticism of taste**

2 **The sense of the beautiful**

3 **Having a love of beauty**

4 **(plural) A branch of philosophy that provides a theory of beauty and the fine arts**

aisthetikos (Greek) pertaining to
sense perception

In common usage, this refers to the large and general sense of a person's taste. Preferences of color, form, content and scale add up to a person's aesthetic.

Taste, in contrast to aesthetics, is a more superficial description of preferences in art. It generally informs the larger issues, but is a more intuitive, sensual response. Aesthetics, while primarily related to sensory perception, can be trained and informed through intellectual processes such as instruction, dialogue and study.

There is an element of culture and experience in aesthetics. While it is probably true that people all over the world equally enjoy a sunset or a bouquet of flowers, we have different ideas about what tastes good, sounds pleasant, and functions best.

SEE:

Abstract	Innovation
Beauty	Originality
Concrete	Synesthesia
Dialogue	Unity
Gestalt	

Anthropomorphic

Anthropomorphic (an-thro-po-MOR-fik)

1 **The attribution of human motivation,
characteristics, or behavior to inanimate
objects, animals, or natural phenomena**

(Greek) anthro (humankind) + morph (form)
= of human form. Biomorphic is a similar
term, but is more general and refers to
anything living

"The worlds about us would be
desolate except for the worlds
within us."

— *Wallace Stevens*

Sometimes designers and artists purposely give human characteristics to their forms, making them angry, soothing, terrifying, and so on. Other times these qualities might be brought by a viewer, who unwittingly wants a work to resemble something familiar.

"Attitude" is a slang term that often conveys a similar notion. I might say, for instance, that a football is a basketball with an attitude. A designer might purposely give an object a reference to a specific attribute, either for humor or satire. A chair, for instance, might be given a form that seems to slouch back on itself, reminding us of a person reclining.

SEE:

Abstract
Content
Ergonomics
Motion

Anticipation

Anticipation (an tis e PA shun)

1 Expectation

2 Foreknowledge, presentiment,
   intuition

antecapere (Latin) = to take before

"The traveler sees what he sees,
the tourist sees what he has come to see."

– Gilbert K. Chesterton

Anticipation often includes pleasant anxiety, the feeling that something is about to happen. In this context, we anticipate a holiday, a party, or a recommended movie. Visually this is related to completion, the tendency of humans to perceive a larger, more harmonious whole. Through anticipation we "fill the blanks" with information that most satisfies or resolves our immediate need. The pleasure is in satisfying; anticipation allows us to prepare for that pleasure and enjoy the resolution.

Because of the way we have been taught to read, our eyes sweep across a page or a picture from left to right. As we scan, we anticipate reaching the end of a line and jumping to the left to start the next. Because of this we rush past or fail to see elements along the right margin. People who read in other directions have different voids.

We've all had occasions when a long-awaited event was less enjoyable than the anticipation. It seems correct that artists, who are, after all, in the business of looking, should help people look ahead.

SEE:

Completion
Dynamic
Emphasis
Gestalt
Integration
Order
Progression

Balance

Balance (BAL encz)

1 A weighing device consisting of a horizontal beam with pans of equal weight on each end

2 A stable state characterized by cancellation of all forces by equal opposing forces

3 A stable mental or psychological state

4 Equality of totals in the credit and debit sides of an account

(Latin) bi (double) + lanx (scale) = having two scales

Our response to balance is intimately linked to our earliest childhood discoveries of our bodies. We instinctively value balance because it is necessary to stand, run, escape. From this primal physical reality we derive our general preference for balance in composition.

Except for brief moments on a roller coaster most people do not want to be off balance. Our sense of balance is so important, in fact, that it is one of the most delicate instruments of our skeletal system. Even a minor ear infection can distort our sense of balance so severely that we are unable to move.

What I dream of is an art of balance, of purity and serenity... something like a good armchair.

– Walt Kelly

In Taoist thought, balancing is the ultimate power and goal of the universe. The symbol for this is the familiar yin-yang, a circle divided into a black and white half, each side curving to penetrate and yield to the other.

Most of us need balance in the large issues of our lives, things like landscape, architecture, diet, and relationships. Perhaps we look to art and design in the same way we enjoy a roller coaster ride—an opportunity to temporarily suspend our sense of balance in a controlled situation. We know the ride will end, and we know we can turn away from the painting if the lack of stability becomes threatening.

The first requisite for balance is control. It is one thing to relinquish balance knowing you can achieve it again and quite another to be out of balance, adrift or askew.

The Navajo word hoz-ro is translated as both beauty and balance. A traditional greeting may be translated as "Go in beauty" or "Walk in balance." This refers to the subtle relationships of man and nature, physical reality and spirit.

In music, balance might be analogous to a regular beat. While this makes an acceptable foundation upon which to build a melody, it has the possibility of becoming boring. Syncopation is one way to move beyond that.

SEE:

Contrast   Order
Duality   Resolution
Dynamic   Tension
Edge   Unity
Figure/Ground

Beauty

1 A pleasing quality associated with harmony form or color; excellence of craftsmanship, truthfulness, originality

2 Appearance or sound that arouses a strong, contemplative delight; loveliness

3 The feature that is most effective, gratifying or telling.

bellus (Latin) = pretty, handsome, fine

> "A thing is not beautiful because it is beautiful, as the he-frog said to the she-frog, it is beautiful because one likes it."
> – Bruno Munari

Though beauty is subjective and culturally influenced, there seem to be some near universal standards. Shrieking noises are not beautiful, cooing sounds almost always will be. A pattern of dots randomly sprinkled on a surface will probably not offend anyone (it is not ugly) but almost no one would call it beautiful. Rounded curvilinear forms are more likely to be considered beautiful than geometric forms.

Some historical periods have defined the artist's job as the creation of beauty. Others see the artist as capturing rather than creating beauty and others think the arts should be no more concerned with beauty than anything else.

Which is the opposite of beautiful – ugly or plain?

SEE:

Balance	Harmony
Confidence	Integrity
Contour	Resolution
Economy	Symmetry
Elegance	Unity

Boundaries separate a "this" from a "that," and a "here" from a "there". A frame around a picture separates the image from the space around it. The frame is a boundary.

The visual strength of a boundary depends on its contrast to adjacent elements. A gray frame on a gray wall will not separate a print from its environment as much as a gold frame, for instance.

The boundaries of a two-dimensional composition are established by the edges of the paper, page or canvas. Rather than specific boundaries like these, three-dimensional work activates a volume of space in its immediate vicinity. This intuitively provides a frame of reference. In order to be called a boundary, the space must be relevant to an observer.

We set boundaries in our personal lives to help us control our relationships, jobs, fears and hopes. These boundaries are usually changeable, like sticks we poke in the ground to mark out a playing field.

Boundary

1 The outer limit, the edge of a shape,
particularly as it stands in relation to an
adjacent form or space

bodina (Latin) = limits; out of bounds means
"past the limits"

"To avoid criticism, do nothing, say nothing, be nothing."

– Elbert Hubbard

SEE:

Closure	Figure/Ground
Contrast	Intersection
Composition	Shape
Edge	Tension
	Center

Center

Center (SEN ter)

1 A point equidistant or at an average
   distance from all points on the outer
   bound aries

2 The middle

3 A point around which something
   revolves; axis

4 The part of an object that is surrounded
   by the rest; core

5 A place of concentrated activity or influence

6 A person or object that is the chief object
   of attention, interest or emotion

7 The ring circling a bull's eye of a target; a
   shot within this ring

Kentron (Greek) = sharp point, stationary
point of a compass

*"Perplexity is
the beginning of
knowledge."*

– Kahlil Gibran

In the traditional "rules" of conventional Western design, the center is considered a static location, and therefore something to be avoided. In other cultural traditions the center is possessed of great power, as for instance in a mandala.

The center of gravity is not necessarily the visual center. It is the specific relationship between an object's center of gravity and the center of the earth that constitutes stability. This is clearly illustrated in architecture, wrestling or dance.

Clay must be centered on the potter's wheel before it can be controlled. This is also true of lathe turning. A gearwheel is generally required to be centered, but there are instances where it is precisely the eccentricity that makes it work.

When a person is stable, balanced, and free of stress we call him or her centered. This is the goal of meditation, yoga, t'ai chi and other personal therapies. Eccentric (off center), as applied to personalities, means colorful, unusual, and therefore interesting.

A familiar danger in drawing is to locate early marks dead center on the page, Creating a visua land emotional gravity that is hard to escape. There's not much happening at the center of a seesaw.

SEE:

Balance   Pattern
Composition   Sentiment
Economy   Structure
Figure/Ground   Tension
Grid   Unity
Order   Closure

Closure

Closure (KLO zher)

1 **The act of closing or the condition of being closed**

2 **Something that closes or shuts**

3 **A finish; conclusion**

clausus (Latin) = enclosed

We have an innate desire to make sense of what we see, and often start by distinguishing "inside" as distinct from "outside". To achieve this we antici- pate and complete a form. By allowing the viewer to complete a form, an artwork establishes a link with the viewer, who becomes part of the process.

( ) We are more likely to read this form as a circle than as two arcs. The enclosed circle is then assigned a contrasting property, for instance, it is "whiter than" or "closer than" other areas of the page. Like magnets, there is a minimum distance that can be bridged by most viewers. Most people will have trouble "closing" this circle (   ).

In relationships we seek an ending (preferably a happy ending) and feel unrest when it doesn't happen. This is an example of our need for resolu- tion. Closure is visual resolution.

"Silence can be an answer."

– Cynthia Copeland Lewis

SEE:

Collaboration

Collaboration (ko lab e RAY shun)

1 **A joint intellectual effort**

2 **Treasonable cooperation with an enemy**

(Latin) com (with) + laborare (work) =
work together

To elaborate is to extend an idea; to co-laborate is to
do so with partners.

In order for a collaboration to work well, dialogue
must be precise throughout the design process.
Definitions are clarified before the dialogue begins,
with the understanding that the improved quality of
the communication will justify time spent in getting
the language clear at the outset.

In a sense all artwork is a collaboration between
form, materials, workmanship, and content.

The candor essential to proper collaboration is a
natural outgrowth of respect between parties.
Respect for ideas mandates a level of clarity that
does justice to the ideas being presented. If I
respect your contribution to a project, I'll persevere
until I fully understand what you're thinking. If I
want your reaction to my ideas, I'll be certain I've
described them accurately.

"Chance favors the prepared mind."

– Louis Pasteur

This kind of dialog, which is inevitable when collaborating with others, can be internalized when working alone. Each of us listens to many voices as we approach a design challenge and we should use the same guidelines of clarity, honesty, and intellectual rigor when we talk to ourselves.

SEE:

Content   Inspiration
Dialogue   Parameters
Dynamic   Sentiment
Emphasis   Symbols
Fragment   Transformation
Icon

Collage

Collage (kol LAJ)

1 An artistic composition of materials
and objects pasted over a surface, often
with unifying lines and color

coller (French) = to paste

"The heart has eyes which
the brain knows nothing of."

– Charles H. Perkhurst

The collage process provides a quick way to explore issues of composition, figure/ground edges, colors and values. Its temporary arrangements are useful to examine the effects of one element upon those around it.

Sometimes the word includes the notion of randomness. Early collage artists dropped pieces of torn paper and glued them to a larger sheet in exactly the pattern in which they fell.

O. B. Hardison, Jr. makes the point that collage is a fitting art form for a culture like ours, in which images flit across our TV screens and sounds of Muzak and traffic collide all around us.

Collage is frequently used as a verb, referring to the process of arranging and overlapping various parts to create a more powerful effect than these elements have as separate units.

SEE:

Balance	Fragment
Composition	Rhythm
Compression	Scale
Contour	Space
Contrast	Structure
Economy	Unity
Figure/Ground	Value

Though composition requires parts, it cannot be considered except as a whole. Composition is to elements as ingredients are to a recipe. You can't make cookies without flour, butter and sugar, but having those ingredients poured into a bowl is a whole lot different than cookies.

Gestalt psychology as applied to visual phenomena identified the fact that humans see the whole before we see the parts. This would suggest that we have a natural tendency toward completeness or harmony.

There are rules of composition just as there are rules of language. In both cases, these are only useful as starting points. The difference between language (which communicates) and gibberish (which does not) is an adherence to fundamental rules. Conventional spelling, pronunciation, grammar and structure do not make communication good—they only make it possible.

Similarly, in visual language, following rules of composition should be seen as a stepping off point, a minimum standard. Here are a few of the rules of composition:

- avoid placement at dead center
- symmetry tends to promote stability
- diagonals are more active than horizontals
- proximity creates tension
- sameness is frequently boring
- regularity creates rhythm
- contrast exaggerates an effect
- placement in corners creates awkward tension
- arches support weight, inverted arches imply weight
- equal amounts of figure and ground confuse the eye

"The arrangements we make are either pleasing or not pleasing. An explanation is not necessary."

– Kenneth Bates

Composition

Composition (kom po ZISH shun)

1 A putting together of parts or elements to form a whole; a combining

2 A short essay; especially one written as a school exercise

3 A settlement by mutual agreement; compromise

The etymological stream traces back to the Latin words com, "with", and ponere, "to place", which gives us compound and expound. A second thread leads back to pose or pause. In the Middle Ages these two words merged to create the sense of "Pause and consider in order to place".

SEE:

Anticipation   Confidence
Completion   Dynamic
Figure/Ground   Gestalt
Positive/Negative Grid

Probably we relate to this because of the physical reality of our experience—we have all been squeezed into an over-packed car, or tucked tightly into bed. Our notions of compression are probably complex and mixed.

In the visual arts, compression can be used to pack energy into a composition. Like a jack in the box, loaded and ready to spring, a picture plane or sculptural space can be "loaded" with ingredients that press against each other to create an exciting energy.

Time is often compressed when we are enjoying ourselves. "Where did the time go?" Cinematically this is indicated by changing the speed, either a dazzling rush of lights zooming past us or a slow-motion effect to suggest that more than usual has been packed into that time.

In some cases compression is an attempt to concentrate as much as possible into a small space. Brandy was invented when ingenious Dutch merchants thought to get more wine across the English Channel in fewer boats by sending it as concentrate and reconstituting it at its destination. Turned out people enjoyed the concentrate.

Compression

Compression (kum PRESH un)

1 The actual or implied sense of forces pressing inward

2 The engine cycle during which gas or vapors are compressed

(Latin) com (together) + premere (to press) = to press together

> "Living is an everyday business.
> Coming to life is strange and beautiful."
>
> – Sister Judith Savard

SEE:

Anthropomorphic
Contrast
Dynamic
Fragment
Interval
Monumentality
Tension

In addition to its idea of solid reality, the word concrete carries a suggestion of bluntness as well. Perhaps this is because of our shared experience of falling, at some time in our lives, on a concrete surface. Not only is this real (that could be said of a grassy hillside too); there is something aggressive about the solidness of concrete.

A concrete image can sometimes provide a valuable point of reference. In a world of ambivalence and contradictions, for instance, concrete advice is welcome. In a disorienting visual composition, a concrete element might provide a necessary anchor.

Concrete poetry is a blend of literary and visual communication. It relies on synesthesia to heighten its power as we simultaneously read words and see an image.

When we think of concrete we probably recall its final state—heavy, hard, and massive. We forget that it was once fluid and could register the imprint of whatever touched it.

Opposites: ethereal, vague, enigmatic.

Concrete

Concrete (kon KRET)

1 Relating to an actual, specific thing or instance; not general

2 Existing in reality or in real experience; perceptible by the senses; real

3 Formed by the coalescence of separate particles or parts into one mass; solid

concretus (Latin) = to grow together, harden

"There is no wisdom like frankness."
    — Benjamin Disraeli

SEE:

Contrast
Density
Economy
Mass
Structure
Transformation
Weight

Confidence

Confidence (KON fi denz)

1 **Trust in a person or thing**

2 **Something confided, such as a secret**

3 **A feeling of assurance or certainty, especially concerning oneself**

confidere (Latin) = com [intensive] + fidere
(to trust)

People present themselves through their walk, their stance, and their gestures. In the same way, a line, form or composition conveys confidence or lack of it. We learn about body language through experience. We see a basketball player stride onto the court, erect and relaxed, then watch him successfully play the game. We learn to associate the gestures with the result.

"They are able because they think they are able."

– Vergil

Confidence is not automatically the result of practice and experience, but it's hard to achieve without practice and experience. A lack of confidence can be a handicap. The same is true of an abundance.

One kind of confidence says "I can do this." Another says, "If I can't do this now, I have the ability to learn."

Pride goes before a fall. But without pride you might not be on your feet in the first place.

SEE:

Anthropomorphic
Dialogue
Dynamic
Resolution
Unity

Content

Content (KON tent)

1 That which is contained in a receptacle

2 Subject matter, as of a speech
or document

3 The meaning or significance of a literary
or artistic work, as distinguished from
its form

4 Ability to receive and hold; capacity

contentus (Latin) = to contain

SEE:

This broad term refers to the message, narrative, meaning or subject of a work. The question often asked of artists, "Where do your ideas come from?" is probably referring to content.

At least in modern thinking, it is rare to describe any content as "inappropriate" for an artist. This shifts emphasis to the accuracy and power of what is being conveyed. Whatever you say, say it with clarity and passion in a way that will have the most effective result.

We use the word "contents" to describe what's inside, as in the contents of a box or the Table of Contents at the beginning of a book.

"The truth is more important than the facts."
— *Frank Lloyd Wright*

Context

1 That which leads up to and follows
  and often specifies the meaning

2 The circumstances in which a
  particular event occurs; a situation

*"There's no where you can be
that isn't where you were meant to be."*

– Lennon and McCartney

Context becomes important in evaluating function, materials, size, etc.

To consider context is to recognize that a work of art or design takes its place in a vast and complicated network of objects and intelligent beings.

It's sometimes more appropriate to change a context than to modify an element.

Just as we sometimes need context to help define a word, physical context is appropriate in evaluating design. The question "Is it good?" should usually be rephrased, "Does it resolve the need here?"

Context is to element as setting is to story.

Note that this word, like texture, derives from weaving. Like the warp and weft of fabric, change a thread here and it will have an effect there. Art isn't necessarily driven by context, but it isn't ignorant of it either.

SEE:

Boundary   Integrity
Composition   Gestalt
Dominance   Pattern
Emphasis   Parameters
Function   Structure
Grouping   Texture
Hierarchy   Tension

Continuity

Continuity (KON te noo e te)

1 An uninterrupted succession,
  unbroken course

2 A detailed shooting script consulted
  to avoid errors from shot to shot in a film

continere (Latin) = to hold together

"As knowledge increases, wonder deepens."

— *Charles Morgan*

Like closure, we subliminally extend lines and forms to seek the largest, most unified whole.

As illustrated in cinematography, continuity is the appearance of a logical and anticipated sequence. A little discontinuity might create interest, but too much will tax believability; our need for order is easily offended.

The less continuity there is in content, the greater the need for visual continuity. A grid used in designing pages for a book is especially important where many diverse images and ideas are being presented.

We seek and see continuity through the rhythms of the seasons, rituals, and cultural traditions. We hang onto a lucky pencil or a childhood toy because it connects us to a valued past.

SEE:

Anticipation
Closure
Gestalt
Grid
Progression
Rhythm

Contour

Contour (KON toor)

1 The outline of a figure, body, or mass

2 A line that represents such an outline

3 A surface, especially of a curving form

contorno (Italian) = to go around, which
derived from con + tornare (Latin) = turn
on a lathe.

When drawing, the outer edge of an object is rendered as a line. Contour lines do not exist in nature, any more than lines of latitude and longitude exist.

Just as lines have a visual speed, we scan an object often by traveling along its contours—skimming along the surface. This process is quick or slow depending on texture, complexity, angles and edges. It is also affected by our level of interest. A car enthusiast will linger over a classic model, where another person would take it in at a glance.

The human brain does most of its work in its surface tissue. To increase the amount of surface a mature brain has increased contours.

A profile, typically a contour from the side, is derived from "to spin a thread forth." Literally it means "as if traced around with a thread."

"Never lose a holy curiosity."

— Albert Einstein

We generally assume that to be "in control" is good and its opposite, "out of control," is a state to be avoided. In the arts, it might be more useful to determine who or what is in control. Is it gravity or the potter in control of the clay as it rotates on the wheel?

There is a difference between surrendering control and not having control. There is a difference between the accomplished painter who allows paint to drip and the child who is still learning about the physics of fluids and gravity. When the Dada artist Jean Arp dropped torn fragments of paper on a larger sheet and glued them where they landed, was he surrendering control?

I am trying to chec my habits of seeing, to counter them for the sa e of greater freshness. I am trying to be unfamiliar with what I'm doing.

— John Cage

Control

1 To exercise authority or dominating influence over

2 To hold in restraint; to chec

3 To verify or regulate by conducting a parallel experiment or by comparing with some other standard

(Latin) contra (against, opposite) + rotulus (roll, as in ledger) [See #3 above]

SEE:
Confidence
Craft
Dialogue
Emphasis
Integration

Contrast clarifies and heightens an effect. To make
a white paper brighter, place a black mark upon it.
Punctuate the silence with a scream, the night with
a candle, and muted tones with a spot of intense
color. Contrast is used to draw attention to an area,
to provide stability or clarity in a composition, and
to affect the figure/ground relationship, either by
clarifying or confusing it.

Contrast can exist in many realms at once. A
thick, jagged, curved black line contrasts
with a thin, smooth, straight red line. We
can simultaneously experience contrast of scale,
value, shape, direction, and surface.

We locate and define ourselves through contrast.
Our first lessons as newborns is to distinguish this
from that, here from there and me from not-me. We
would be lost without contrasts, snow-blind in a
universe barren of distinctions.

Visual, aural and olfactory contrasts are instinctive.
You don't need to be taught what is a good smell or
a bad smell. Other contrasts are learned because of
cultural norms or associations.

SEE:

Contrast (KON trast)

1 To set in opposition in order to show or emphasize differences

2 A striking dissimilarity between things being compared

3 The use of opposing elements such as colors, forms or lines in proximity to produce an intensified effect

(Latin) contra (against) + stare (to stand) = to strive against

"If you want someone to listen to what you're saying, whisper it."

—Cynthia Copeland Lewis

Craft

Craft (kraft)

1 Skill or ability in something, especially in handwork or the arts; proficiency, expertness

2 Skill in evasion or deception; cunning; guile

craft (Middle English) = strength, skill, device

SEE:

Confidence
Control
Function
Integrity
Join
Unity

In its first sense, craft refers to the quality of anything that is made. A painting, a building or a meal may be well crafted. Usually excellent craftsmanship is the result of talent, training, and experience.

The pleasure of good craftsmanship is universal, transcending language, culture, and time.

A more specific use of this word refers to objects of a principally utilitarian origin, as in "handicrafts" such as furniture, textiles, metalwork, and so on. This double use of the word can be confusing and requires care: not all crafts are well-crafted, and most fine art relies on its craft. (Read that again until it makes sense.)

A good idea poorly realized because of a lack of craft is like a song poorly sung—a nagging disappointment.

"The work of craft is a fine example of the work of life, our universal obligation."

— Carla Needleman

Critique

Critique (kri TEK)

1 **A critical review or commentary, especially dealing with art**

2 **A critical discussion of a specific topic**

3 **The art of criticism**

kritikos (Greek) = able to discern, from kritos, to separate, or choose

A critique, or crit, for short, is a staple part of an art education. It is a chance to examine work in a unique situation, pulled out, or separated from usual experience for this focused evaluation.

There are many forces at work in critique—the culture of the maker, the culture of the viewer, the language of the critic, the context of the viewing, and so on. A critique should be a dialogue that encourages participation from all interested parties. In some cases this is a literal dialogue, or conversation between participants. Even when this is not the case, of for instance when a critique is published in a magazine, a responsible reader will "talk back" to the critic as a means of clarifying personal opinions. Because criticism is largely (but not entirely) based

SEE:

Beauty
Collaboration
Confidence
Craft
Dialogue
Eclectic
Originality

on comparison, critique must take place within a context. To say, "This is good" begs the question, "Compared to what?" or "Good for what?" We critique, say, Michelangelo's paintings and find them to be good, within the unspoken parameters of Western ideals of the human figure, a Renaissance understanding of Christianity, and the confines of his medium.

Though one meaning of criticism has a negative connotation ("You're always criticizing me!") the more common use does not imply a negative response, but simply a straightforward, deliberate consideration of the value of a work. A critic is not a person who doesn't like anything, but a person with special skills of evaluation.

"'Tis with our judgments as our watches, none Go just alike, yet each believes his own."

—Alexander Pope

Decorative

Decorative (DEK er e tiv)

1 **Serving to decorate; ornamental**

2 **That which invests with an honor**

decorare (Latin) = to ornament

Often used in the pejorative (negative) sense of unnecessary embellishment, arbitrarily applied to an object without regard to its form.

Decorative additions are frosting on a cake: sometimes used to camouflage mistakes in what lies beneath, and sometimes appropriate additions that elevate what was good to something outstanding.

In Eastern aesthetics, decoration is a testament of devotion. Hindu temples and Muslim mosques, for instance, are dazzling monuments to decoration. In their approach, it would be impossible to have too much decoration, just as it would be impossible to have too much devotion to god.

"God lives in the details."
— *Mies van der Rohe*

SEE:

Density

1 **The degree to which anything is filled or occupied**

2 **The amount of something per unit measure**

3 **Thickness of consistency; impenetrability**

densus (Latin) = thick, crowded

Density can be used to indicate stability, weight, or a sense of movement. It also brings an opportunity for contrast—"more dense" contrasts with "less dense". These are, of course, relative measures.

Though usually a visual term, we can apply the concept of density to other situations. For instance, some works are more dense with meaning than others. In some contexts, like underbrush and poetry, dense might translate to impenetrable.

Density refers to the effect of locating elements close to each other. It is a way of creating shade with a single, fixed-value mark such as a dot of ink that is always the same black. An example is the Benday pattern used to reproduce photos in newspaper printing.

"When you cannot make up your mind which of two evenly balanced courses of action you should take—choose the bolder."

– W. J. Slim

SEE:

Compression	Proximity
Contrast	Ratio
Dominance	Scale
Emphasis	Value
Hierarchy	Weight

Design

Design (d ZIN)

1 To conceive, invent, contrive

2 To form a plan for

3 To draw a sketch

4 To have as a goal or purpose, to intend

5 A visual composition, pattern

6 A reasoned purpose, intention

(Latin) de (out) + signare (mark) = mark out, designate

SEE:

Everything!

"Design is the conscious and intuitive effort to impose meaningful order."

—Victor Papanek

This word is both noun and verb. When we attempt to arrange parts in a way that is most efficient, attractive and/or meaningful, we are engaged in the process of design. The result of the activity, which may be an intellectual property as well as a sketch or model, is also called a design.

As verb, design refers to a human activity. We don't think of nature as designing, though we often see configurations in nature that we call design. The process of design is rooted in intention. Nature develops forms to achieve certain ends (the egg to protect the chick) but not because an intellect decided this would be best. In this example, the stimulus was the continuation of the species, which as far as we can tell is a component of the natural world.

As a creative act, design is related to innovation in other fields, such as literature, music, and science. Nevertheless, subtle shades of difference are built into the language. We do not speak of designing a symphony, an equation or a novel, anymore than we compose a building.

" He who does not understand your silence
will probably not understand your words."

— Elbert Hubbard

SEE:

Balance	Figure/Ground
Center	Gestalt
Collaboration	Hierarchy
Control	Join
Dominance	Progression
Emphasis	Tension

Dialogue

Dialogue (DI a log)

1 **A conversation between two or more people**

2 **An exchange of ideas or opinions**

3 **Lines in a play**

(Greek) dia (between) + logos (speech) = conversation

Just as it is annoying to simultaneously hear two unrelated conversations or two radios playing different stations, an unpleasant tension is created when the elements of a composition don't relate to each other.

A dialogue is not the same as two monologues going on in sequence. In genuine dialogue there must be a period of assimilation as information is received and considered. Listening is an important part of dialogue. In the design process this translates to taking a step back from a work in progress.

In a work, dialogue might refer to cross-reference between elements—a texture, hue, value or shape might indicate an association or relationship between parts.

In some contexts, such as a medieval cathedral or a contemporary urban installation, art seeks to involve viewers, while other situations, like most museums, present artwork as a completed result of an essentially private experience.

Dissonance

Dissonance (DIS e nenz)

1 **Harsh or inharmonious in sound;
   discordant**

2 **Disagreeing or at variance**

(Latin) dis (apart) + sonare (to sound) =
inharmonious sound

If the effect of harmony is to create a sense of resolution, beauty and order, the result of dissonance (its opposite) is to create tension, contrast, and lack of resolution.

In cooking, a sour taste is sometimes used to make a sweetness more pronounced. In music, a dissonant passage introduces discomfort that forces the listener to be more aware of the sounds as he struggles to find order. It then makes the perception of harmony all the more pronounced if it returns.

Harmony is to soaring as dissonance is to falling.

"We design, and we have designs on. Maybe the difference is between discovering order and imposing order. I think the former is a good thing, and the latter isn't, necessarily."

— Robley Wilson, Jr.

Dominance

Dominance (DOM e nens)

1 Preeminence in position or prevalence;
  ascendancy

2 The tendency for one element or group to
  command greater attention than another

dominans (Latin) = commanding, ruling

Dominance can be achieved by size, value, color, shape or position. If several of these factors are combined the effect will be more pronounced. A large bright object in the middle of a page will dominate most everything else.

If these factors are used in contradiction (a large dynamic shape overlapped by smaller, less interesting ones) the result could be an appealing tension or a confusing irritation.

Some forms present a clear dominance; for instance, the Washington Monument is dominantly vertical. In other instances the components and attributes of a work are similar enough that there is no clear dominance.

If a composition is unsuccessful, the problem might not be the wrong choice of element, just incorrect dominance.

"There is no such thing as empty space; there's always something to see."

— John Cage

Dynamic

Dynamic (dy NAM ik)

1 Pertaining to energy, force or motion related to force

2 Characterized by continuous change

3 Energizing, vigorous, forceful

4 Variation of intensity, as in a musical sound

dynamikos (Greek) = powerful, strong

"My imagination takes its strength and guides its direction from what I see and hear and learn and feel and remember of my living world."

— Eudora Welty

Because motion always requires time, the appearance or sense of motion in a stable work will extend its impact. A composition that implies movement, that is, a dynamic composition, is more likely to grab our attention than a static one.

In a dynamic situation the individual elements are interrelated, like players on a football field. The location and activity of one member of the team affects the options and responsibilities of every other member. This is an example of a dynamic system. Every component of a successful design is linked to every other in a similar way.

SEE:

Center   Motion
Compression   Rhythm
Contrast   Synesthesia
Dissonance   Tension
Intersection

Eclectic

Eclectic (i KLEK tik)

1 To choose the best from diverse sources, systems or styles

eklektikos (Greek) = selecting

When working within an established tradition, compatible ingredients have already been identified. An architect planning a colonial style house has a limited menu of detail elements from which to select, in some ways making his job easier. Artists working eclectically must be better informed and more sensitive in order to make appropriate choices.

The challenge of an eclectic style lies in defining what's best, determining the particulars of arrangement, and bringing the results to a physical reality. In the truest sense of the word, this describes the task of the arts: to select, assemble, and arrange the best parts of all that there is.

"Do what you can, with what you have, where you are"

— Theodore Roosevelt

SEE:

Economy

Economy (i KON e me)

1 The careful or thrifty use of resources

2 The management of the resources of a country, community or business

oikonomos (Greek) house + managing

In addition to the usual association with money this word means "the functional arrangement of elements within a structure or system". It derives from a combination of the Greek words for "house" and "managing"—economy is a matter of getting the most from given resources while keeping the house in order.

"*Everything should be made as simple as possible, but not simpler.*"

– Albert Einstein

SEE:

Balance
Context
Contrast
Dynamic
Emphasis
Fragment
Unity

Edge

edge (ej)

1 **The usually thin, sharpened side of a blade, weapon, or tool**

2 **Keenness, as of desire or enjoyment; zest**

3 **A rim, brink or crest**

4 **A dividing line or point of transition; a margin, a border**

egge (Middle English) = edge, point, or sword. There might be connections with ancient words for ax, tool, spike, and tart, as in a sharp taste

Edges are usually active places. In a crowd, though the focus might be on what's happening at the center, it is at the edge that there is movement and the possibility for freedom. People in the center of a throng have little choice except to be carried along, but those at the edge can wander off.

Center equates with stability, edges with instability. In the center of a room, we are surrounded by equal spaces. We have room to shift without losing our bearings. A mark in the center of a page is not at risk of being overlooked. It is at risk, however, of being boring. The center is comfortable; the edge is threatening or exhilarating, depending on your personality.

In a two-dimensional composition, marks at the center are locked into relationships with the other marks on the page. Marks near the edge split their allegiance between other marks and the edge itself; they know where the paper ends.

An edge is to a line as a scent is to a flower.

Edges are given their power by their relative proximity. A curb is less threatening than the molding that surrounds the edge of a roof, though both might be of the same width. The difference is in the distance between this edge and the next-closest surface. A rim on a bowl is different in the same way from the rim of a plate. In three-dimensional form, edges are given their power not only by their direction and shape, but by their relationship to the next-closest form.

Edge is a word most commonly seen in the singular. Of course objects have many edges, but there is more drama in the edge of a knife than in the edges of a saw.

People who live dangerously are said to live "on the edge." They are in a position of almost falling off, of crossing over, of shifting allegiance. A fearful person is described as "edgy."

> *Design can be on turbid days what sonar is to bats at night. It is a way to transmit signs, to ricochet symbols outside ourselves, and by that to locate the edges of things.*

– *Roy Behrens*

SEE:

Center	Intersection
Composition	Interval
Contour	Join
Contrast	Scale
Economy	Tension
Figure/Ground	Elegance
Gestalt	

*"Don't look for meaning in the
words. Listen to the silences."*
-Samuel Beckett

Elegance

1 **Refinement and grace in movement, appearance or manners**

2 **Tasteful opulence in form, decoration or presentation**

eligere (Latin) = select or choose

This term implies the best of the best. Beautiful is different from ugly, but elegant is the most beautiful of the group.

There is a sense of economy in elegance. We use this word to describe the reduced, essential movements of an athlete, or a melody stripped of anything extraneous. In science, a solution that resolves inconsistencies without complex artifice is called an elegant solution.

Emphasis

Emphasis (EM fa sis)

1 Special importance or significance placed upon or imparted to something

2 Stress applied to a syllable, word or passage by the use of a gesture or other indication

3 Force or intensity of expression, feeling or action

4 Sharpness or vividness of outline, prominence

emphainein (Greek) = to exhibit; in language, to express more than the words alone convey

SEE:

Emphasis is to composition what gesture is to conversation.

Emphasis is a kindly hint from artist to viewer, a clue that assists in understanding a work. It follows that it is less necessary in obvious compositions and more necessary in subtle or complex ones. The sentence "Run for your life!" doesn't need to be underlined; the message is clear.

As in so many other situations, this factor can be judiciously "not used" to create or enlarge an effect. The paintings of Jackson Pollock derive their power from (among other things) their lack of emphasis. Parallels can be found in modern drama and music.

"Whatever feeling, whatever state you have at the time of making the line will register in the stroke."

– Robert Henri

Entropy

Entropy (EN tre pe)

1 **A measure of the capacity of a system to undergo spontaneous change**

2 **A measure of the randomness, disorder, or chaos in a system**

entropie (Greek) = turning or change

SEE:

Balance	Order
Dissonance	Resolution
Distort	Structure
Fragment	Tension
Integration	

The Second Law of Thermodynamics states that nature tends toward entropy. If you drop a handful of marbles, they are more likely to scatter than to end up in a single pile on the floor.

This is in a way the reverse side of gestalt, which refers to the human tendency to visually assemble parts into a coherent whole. Order in the arts (representation, precision, control) is evidence of our apparent control over chaos. Others will argue that art is at its best when it connects with the randomness of life, describing it by yielding to it.

"Even a brick wants to be something."

– Louis Kahn

Ergonomics

Ergonomics (ur go NOM iks)

1 The applied science of equipment design, as for the workplace, intended to maximize productivity by reducing operator fatigue and discomfort; also called biotechnology, human engineering, human factors engineering

2 Design factors, as for the workplace, intended to maximize productivity by minimizing operator fatigue and discomfort

3 The study of the behavior of groups of muscles, with the assumption of seeking the most efficient or least harmful application of those muscles; a tool handle that takes best advantage of leverage while minimizing strain would be called "ergonomically correct"

(Greek) ergon (work) + nomos (law) = proper work, best method

SEE:

Anthropomorphic	Dynamic
Balance	Ecology
Center	Function
Composition	Organic
Confidence	Unity

Ergonomics is a specific branch of functionalism that relies on scientifically gathered information about the human form and the way it moves. Where function can be broadly interpreted, the angles and range of movement of an elbow or a knee can be objectively measured. This merges the roles of scientist, designer, and physician.

"Originality is nothing but judicious imitation."

— John Cage

Figure/Ground

Figure (FIG yer)

1 **The outline, form or silhouette of a thing**

Ground (ground)

1 **A surrounding area; background**

Figure/ground refers to the relationship between what stands forward and what recedes in a composition. On this page, the letters are figure and the white of the paper constitutes the ground. The degree of tension or harmony between figure and ground contributes significantly to the effect of a work.

The three-dimensional equivalent of figure/ground is positive/negative.

Through understanding and use of unusual figure/ground relationships, art work is generally made more interesting. If the amounts of figure and ground are approximately equal, the effect can be confusing to the eye, which jumps back and forth between two conflicting options. A familiar example of this is the optical illusion in which an image can be interpreted as a chalice or as two heads in profile.

The near-balance of figure and ground (known as binary) animates a composition and is often used in posters, highway signs and similar eye-grabbing situations. This push/pull energy can make a complex composition too distracting to enjoy.

When figure dominates ground the effect is clear but potentially boring. Locating a clearly outlined object in the center of a page leaves no doubt about the subject, but the presentation lacks subtlety, charm and elegance.

SEE:

Balance	Grouping
Boundary	Hierarchy
Contrast	Integrity
Dominance	Positive/Negative
Dynamic	Space
Edge	Structure
Emphasis	Tension
	Unity

Formal

Formal (FOR mul)

1 Pertaining to the essential form or
constitution of something, in the same
sense that "structural' refers to structure.
In discussions of art, this refers to
information received on a visual level, as
distinct from issues of content or meaning

forma (Latin) = contour or shape

Form is best understood as distinct from something else, such as surface. A grapefruit, for instance, can be described by its color, surface, scale, context, etc. Of course it can be described by scientists, nutritionists and fruit growers in ways particular to the interests of each. To identify it as a sphere addresses its 'formal' qualities.

Form, like structure, is usually a fundamental aspect of a solid object. You can paint a grapefruit, or suspend it by a thread, or set it in the middle of a stadium but it will always, formally, be a sphere. Because of this, form is important to all design, a common denominator that separates the average from the exceptional. Superb decoration, craftsmanship, and exquisite materials on a mediocre form will yield a disappointing result.

This word conveys overtones of correctness as in "formal dress" with its air of a specific code of proper breeding, or what are called formal modes of address, such as "Your Honor".

To provide uniform information we fill out forms. A uniform is a universal form, a common identification that relies on shapes, color, and decoration for communication.

"The principal mark of genius is not perfection but originality."

— Arthur Koestler

SEE:

Anthropomorphic	Fragment
Compression	Organic
Dynamic	Shape
Edge	Volume
Figure/Ground	

Fragment

Fragment (FRAG ment)

1 A part broken off or detached from the whole

2 Something incomplete; an odd bit or piece

3 To break up into fragments, fragmentize

fragmentum (Latin) = broken

SEE:

Compression   Integration
Contrast   Join
Distort   Tension
Emphasis   Unity
Gestalt

In order for an object or form to be perceived as a fragment there must be a clear sense of a whole. This can be a learned association; most people can identify a fragment of broken crockery because of previous familiarity with intact cups and bowls.

There is an instinctive tendency in humans to establish a relationship between elements wherever possible. Even subtle clues are often sufficient to trigger connections between one unit and another. If there is a size difference, the smaller piece becomes the fragment.

Fragment implies a passage of time... Then it was whole, now it is in pieces.

Fragment as verb implies a sectioning off, usually as an undesirable thing to do. A composition might be fragmented by adding a line or introducing a color. Unity, the opposite of fragmentation, is more commonly preferred.

When continuity is expected, fragmentation is easier to achieve and more disruptive. A piece cut from a checkerboard will read as a fragment, but the same size piece pulled from an abstract pattern might seem complete.

Fragments introduce the notion of mystery or puzzle-solving. A fragment of a conversation ("after the balloons and rubber chickens arrived...") can be more intriguing than the complete thought.

> "Discontinuity and fragmentation are part of the deep structure of modern culture."
>
> – O.B. Hardison, Jr.

An obvious use of function in design is as a solution to a specific problem. The function of a cup is to hold liquid, etc. But defining function is rarely as easy as that. Is the function of a chair to support weight, ornament a room, or display the taste of the owner? Probably all that and more. And to make things more complicated, these functions will change depending on context.

In mathematics the way a number acts upon another number is called its function. Adding, subtracting, multiplying and dividing are functions. We also use the word to describe a relationship between elements, as in: "His power is a function of his wealth." Or in a visual example, "That texture is a function of repetition."

> "Nothing is beautiful that is not useful; nothing is useful that is not beautiful."
>
> – Japanese saying

Function

1 The natural or proper action for which a person, office, or mechanism is fitted

2 To serve in a proper or appropriate manner

3 Something closely related to another thing and dependent upon it for its existence, value or significance

fungi (Latin) = to perform

The sculptor Horatio Greenough said, "form follows function." First identify what needs to happen, then satisfy that need in a way that makes best use of materials, space, and resources. The result, he reasoned, is automatically the correct form.

Function can be inferred from association. Objects may look like tools or toys, even though they don't function as such, if they use a formal vocabulary associated with those functions.

If the function of a greenhouse is to raise plants, what is the function of a shrine?

SEE:

Context
Ergonomics
Grid
Hierarchy
Invention

Order
Pattern
Structure
Unity

Gestalt

Gestalt (ge STALT)

1 A unified physical, psychological or symbolic configuration having properties that cannot be derived from its parts

2 A branch of psychology developed in the 1920's that says patterns can only be understood as unified wholes and not by examining their parts

gestalt (German) = form or shape

SEE:

Closure	Integration
Context	Negative/Positive
Economy	Resolution
Figure/Ground	Structure
Fragment	Transformation
Harmony	Unity

This concept is borrowed by the visual arts to describe the phenomenon that images are perceived as unified wholes before they are perceived as parts. Our need for wholeness is so great we assemble elements into as large a unit as possible. We will see a row of dots as a dotted line rather than a collection of small marks.

When confronted with an image or form that lacks unity, a viewer finds the effect unrelated, busy or disturbing.

A knowledge of gestalt allows a designer to leave forms unconnected, knowing that a viewer will add the missing ingredients to create a unified whole This makes it possible to hint rather than state, to involve viewers as participants in the act of viewing. We enjoy finding the Big Dipper in the starry night sky because of the effort we bring to the process.

Perhaps the most radical change that has occurred in the history of theoretical thinking is the switch from the atomistic conception of the world as an assembly of circumscribed things to that of a world of forces acting in the dimension of time. These forces are bound to organize themselves in fields, interacting, grouping, connecting, fusing, and separating.

— Rudolf Arnheim

Gesture

Gesture (JES chur)

1 A motion of the body made to express
   thoughts and emotions, or to emphasize
   speech.

2 To show, express or direct by movements

   gestura (Latin) = mode of action

You can recognize a friend's walk from a block away; what does that tell us about the importance of gesture? As any mime will tell you (if you can get him to talk), capture the gesture and you have captured the personality.

Gesture combines our given physiognomy with our learned movements—the length of our arm with the boldness of our stroke.

Gesture is similar to attitude. Gestures can be coarse, abrupt, soothing, angry, and so on. Gesture has a lot to do with signature.

Medium affects gesture. A loose spontaneous gesture might be best captured in paint. The same gesture might be diminished—starved to death—by a pencil.

A physical gesture is the collection of movement, form and pace. In the visual arts, we can use the same word to describe the subtle but essential qualities that result from a particular action by a particular person at a specific time.

A series of alignments and intersections, grids can be used to assemble, organize or separate elements. They can be seen or inferred.

Because of its mathematical origin, a grid is "transparent," meaning it can be understood without language. In a city laid out on a grid, a couple of fingers and a little pointing can direct a stranger to a destination.

Grids are used to reduce or enlarge an image. They simplify a mathematical relationship. Digitization, which has revolutionized our media, uses a grid.

SEE:

Grid

1 A framework of parallel or crisscrossed bars; gridiron

2 A pattern of horizontal and vertical lines forming squares of uniform size on a map, chart, or aerial photograph, used as a reference for locating points

Short for gridiron, the flat framework of parallel metal bars used for broiling meat or fish, from gredil (Middle English) = griddle

In mathematics, cartography, and bingo a grid is a locating device.

Cities are sometimes designed on a grid because the logical system can be translated from large to small scale without loss of information. Whether you are going to the next block or across town, the grid will allow the language of directions to be consistent. If you can find your way around the block, you can find your way across town.

"It is respectable to have no illusions, and safe, and profitable and dull."
– Joseph Conrad

The human perceptive apparatus has an inherent tendency to assemble visual information into groups. Enter a room for the first time and you will group the furniture and decorations into clusters. If the process is facilitated by having small collections associated by proximity, shape or color, the room will intuitively feel more comfortable.

Artists use grouping to convey subtle messages and to guide a viewer through a piece.

"Like takes to like."

— Homer

Grouping

Grouping (GROO ping)

1 **The act or process of arranging in groups**

2 **A collection of objects arranged in a group**

gruppo (Italian) = knot

Elements are commonly grouped by

similarity	-	size, color, shape, textures, etc.
proximity	-	close, touching, overlapping
orientation	-	visual or psychological

Harmony

Harmony (HAR mo ne)

1 Agreement in feeling, approach, action, disposition; sympathy; accord

2 The pleasing interaction or appropriate combination of the elements in a whole

3 A mutually beneficial relationship between parts

4 The effect of various parts supporting, augmenting or complementing each other

harmos (Greek) = joint

From the Greek word for joint, connoting the way parts are joined together. A lack of harmony is described as being "out of joint."

People like harmony.

In music, harmony is central to the traditional barbershop quartet. Each of the four voices handles the melody in a unique way, but always in such a manner that every resulting chord is balanced, modulated and complete. The result is almost irresistible richness for a song or two, but becomes predictable and saccharine before long. That's harmony for you.

"I want to start living my life in grace and harmony. "

– Kurt Vonnegut, Jr.

Harmony [with etymological roots in the joinery of wood-working] is a basic principle in Greek and Oriental philosophy. Note that both the Greeks and Indians have a carpenter God; the son of the Christian God was also a carpenter. The fact that wood is the primary life-stuff "of which all things are made" reveals the mythical necessity that the god be referred to as a carpenter.

Dictionary of Word Origins

SEE:

Balance	Join
Center	Order
Composition	Organic
Contrast	Resolution
Dissonance	Unity
Fragment	

Hierarchy

Hierarchy (hi e RAR ke)

1 **A body of elements arranged according to rank, authority or capacity**

2 **A body of entities arranged in a graded series**

3 **Clergy arranged in successive ranks**

hierarkhia (Greek) = the power of a priest, from hieros (sacred, supernatural)

In the visual arts, hierarchy is the presentation of certain elements as more important than others. By conveying a clear sense of hierarchy an artist provides stability, sequence, and movement within a design.

In the absence of hierarchy, a viewer feels lost and ill at ease. A determined viewer might respond by creating a hierarchy, or by looking for subtle clues that were missed in the first viewing. Most will move on.

Hierarchy can be established by any of the devices in the artist's repertoire—position, value, form, contrast, rhythm, etc.

The time-honored tricks to test hierarchy are to either turn a composition upside-down, or stand back and squint. Though apparently childish, these devices show the eye not what it "thinks" is most obvious, but what really is most obvious.

*"We think in generalities,
but we live in detail."*

– *Walt Kelly*

Most commonly, this refers to the "color" of a color, that which, for instance, we call red. The hue is then modified by saturation, value, tint, or shade, as in bright red, dull red, and so on.

It is often useful to speak of the temperature of a color. This might have a reference to genuine temperature, such as red, which is the color of glowing embers and is a hot color, but mostly it is an intuitive scale that identifies an optic quality that is different from value and saturation.

Hue

Hue (hyoo)

1 The dimension of color that refers to a
   scale of perceptions ranging from red
   through yellow, green, blue and circularly,
   back to red (Got it?)

2 A particular gradation of colors; tint; shade

3 Character; aspect

hewe (Old English) = complexion;
                              appearance

" Computers are useless. They only give answers. "

    – Pablo Picasso

SEE:
Contrast
Emphasis
Harmony
Value

Icon

Icon (I kon)

1 An image, representation

2 A simile or symbol

3 A representation or picture of a
   sacred Christian personage, itself
   regarded as sacred

eikon (Greek) = likeness or image

*"Good design is whatever addresses the need a
society has for an image of itself.*

— Gilbert K. Chesterton

An icon is a graphic symbol of almost universal nature—a visual shorthand that is understood by most members of a community.

In the creation of words, when a sound suggests its meaning the effect is called onomatopoeia (e.g., "whoosh"). A visual equivalent would be a stylized picture such as a circle with radiating lines to indicate the sun. Such words and symbols often transcend culture and specific language. Other icons are culture dependent – my computer screen has a small drawing that will make no sense to a person who has never used a file folder.

Icons enlarge communication within the community of viewers who understand them ("A picture says a thousand words") but alienate those who do not.

The adverb version is <u>iconic</u> as in "The artists used iconic structures like domes and towers as sexual references."

SEE:

Anthropomorphic   Fragment
Content   Repetition
Economy   Sentiment
Emphasis   Symbol

Parts can relate through their differences (contrast) as well as their similarities (harmony).

In society, integration is achieved not when all cultures have given up their uniqueness, but when all elements can celebrate what sets them apart. Similarly, a composition does not seek to homogenize all its elements, but to create an environment (structure) that will accommodate the unique contributions of each.

The Latin word for "<u>hearth</u>" is focus. In usage, this is the center of a household, or the common gathering area. This reminds us that integration requires that we not lose focus. Hierarchy and unity are essential to, and the result of, integration.

"Sight is a promiscuous sense. The avid gaze always wants more."

— *Susan Sontag*

Integration

Integration (in te GRA shun)

1 The resulting whole made by bringing all parts together; unification

2 The organization of organic, psychological or social traits and tendencies of a personality into a harmonious whole

3 Desegregation; a successful relationship of elements

integrare (Latin) = to make complete (from integer, a whole number)

SEE:

Balance   Hierarchy
Collaboration   Join
Composition   Organic
Contrast   Pattern
Emphasis   Resolution
Harmony   Unity

Integrity

Integrity (in TEG re te)

1 Rigid adherence to a code of behavior

2 To remain consistent with larger, often moral, dictates

3 The state of being unimpaired; soundness

4 Completeness; unity

integritas (Latin) = completeness; purity

"Every artist knows that he is engaged in an encounter with infinity, and that work done with heart and hand is ultimately worship of Life itself."

— Sôetsu Yanagi

SEE:

Boundary   Resolution
Content   Sentiment
Dialogue   Stylization
Originality   Unity
Parameters

In visual composition, it is sometimes possible to resolve compositional dilemmas by sacrificing or diluting certain elements. This is done at the expense of integrity. We are surrounded by examples of this sort of compromise, from elevator music to package design to hotel decoration. It is the result of an attempt to offend no one, and usually results in a look that is as undemanding and ultimately uninteresting as it is inoffensive.

This is not to imply that all work of integrity offends someone, and certainly not that all offensive work is inherently noble. The thousands of decisions that go into the creation of a work of art or design must eventually be tested against some yardstick. It is in the selection of this measure that an artist defines his or her integrity.

Integer: A single unit; from this, integrate, to make into a whole.

A field test of integrity is the If-I-remove-this-does-the-piece-suffer? game. In a fully integrated design there is nothing extraneous.

When freedom of expression is threatened, an artist with integrity will stand by his or her work. Too often, however, meaningful criticism is ignored by an artist who hides behind the cloak of protecting a presumed integrity.

In the same way that moral integrity means staying true to a philosophy, visual integrity is the result of remaining consistent to a concept or approach.

Intersection

Intersection (in ter SEK shun)

1 **A place where two or more roads cross**

2 **The point common to two or more geometric figures**

(Latin) inter (mutually) + secare
(to cut) = mutually cut

The crossing point of two lines, forms or movements. Typically a stable point.

"X" marks the spot.

In driving, intersect equals opportunity, the chance to change course. That's where you're most likely to encounter a sign.

In the truest sense, this term refers to a measure, the "section" from one parallel line to its next closest line. We use this notation in cities, where we describe the distance covered in terms of blocks. We could as justly call these intersections.

Intersections can be actual or anticipated. Two sloped lines climbing a page might not actually cross, but we extend them in our imagination to create an intersection. There is likely to be a sense of completion or resolution associated with this subconscious activity.

"To be a master of the metaphor is a sign of genius, because a good metaphor implies an intuitive perception of similarity between dissimilar things."

— Aristotle

"I'm getting better at playing the silences."

— Glenn Gould

SEE:

Compression	Pattern
Intersection	Figure/Ground
Grid	Positive/Negative
Rhythm	Tension

Interval

1 **A space between two objects, points or units**

2 **The temporal duration between two specified instants, events or states**

3 **An intermission**

(Latin) inter (between) + vallum (ramparts) = between stations

Just as there is a specific gap that defines the attracting range between two magnets, there is a "normal" interval that seems correct for each visual arrangement. If this interval is too large, the elements drift apart and create an unresolved composition. If it is too small, the effect is compressed space, often with a corresponding tension.

An interval is the visual equivalent of a "rest" in musical notation.

When trying to cross a brook, you look for the size of the stepping stones and the distance between them. Just as this interval is related to your physical size (the length of your stride) we each have slightly different notions about interval that probably relate to our bodies and our social environment.

We seem to have an intuitive sense of an "incorrect" interval:

• *in time (an uncomfortable pause before speaking)*

• *in two-dimensional space*
(letters awkw a r dly spaced)

• *in three-dimensional space*
(furniture crowded together or too spread out)

Intuition

Intuition (in too ISH n)

1 **Knowing without the use of rational processes; immediate cognition**

2 **A sense of something not evident or deducible**

3 **A capacity for guessing accurately; sharp insight**

intueri (Latin) = to look toward

Intuition is the saving grace that prevents art from being reduced to formula. It is the charming stumble, the rebellious bellow, the step off into the dark.

Intuition is what we know automatically, without having learned it. We can't improve our intuition, but we can improve our ability to listen to it and to trust it.

Intuition is the tool that lets us cross-reference our senses. Through it we know how to cool down a hot color or quiet a noisy composition.

Intuition can't be shared but it can be communicated.

"If I have ever made any valuable discoveries, it has been owing more to patient attention, than to any other talent."

— *Isaac Newton*

SEE:

Balance	Organic
Center	Sensuous
Confidence	Synesthesia
Context	Proportion
Gestalt	Unity

Invention

Invention (in VEN shun)

1 **A new device or process developed from study and experimentation**

2 **A mental fabrication; falsehood**

inventus (Latin) = to come upon

In common usage the word carries a sense of mechanics; a semi-logical, probably sequential process of problem-solving. We speak of inventing a mousetrap, but not a sculpture.

In the arts, invention often refers to the creation of a device or apparatus or concept that is then put to use in a range of situations. An artist might invent a visual language that is used to compose a work.

"There is nothing new in art except talent."

– Anton Chekov

SEE:

Collaboration
Dialogue
Economy
Function
Innovation
Template

The root meaning of "art" is "to join, or fit together."

Joinery imposes a relationship. Picture the difference between a book set upon a table and a book nailed to a table.

Kinds of Joins:

permanent	–	temporary
obvious	–	subtle
familiar	–	exotic
integral	–	superficial
organic	–	mechanical

The word joinery can relate specifically to a physical joint (for instance, a mortise and tenon) or to the effect created. The components of a tree illustrate a specific type of joinery. The joinery displayed in an insect, by contrast, is altogether different.

Joinery can create sequence:
trunk —> limb —> branch —> twig —> bud

The knees of a wooden boat, an area of critical joining inside the hull, are made from that part of a tree where a limb grows out of the trunk because the structure of that wood was, literally, made to be a joint.

Join

Join (joyn)

1 Putting or bringing together, uniting or making continuous

2 Putting or bringing into close association or relationship

3 The way elements are attached to each other

jungere (Latin) = skeleton joint or junction

"God made everything out of nothing.
But the nothingness shows through."

– Paul Valéry

SEE:

Collaboration   Order
Economy   Organic
Fragment   Structure
Harmony   Unity
Mass

Line

Line (lyn)

1 The locus of a point having one degree
   of freedom

2 A thin, continuous mark, as that made
   by a pen, pencil or brush applied to
   a surface

3 An indentation or crease in the skin;
   a wrinkle

linum (Latin) = thread, derived from
                the word for flax

SEE:

Lines are a human invention: they are intellectual constructs to impose order such as in a line of thought, or a line of flight. In the visual world, lines are generally a shorthand for edges. We perceive objects because of the dozens of ways they differ from their surroundings. We abbreviate these differences by drawing a contour line.

Famous Lines: the Equator, the horizon, the line of sight, the Mason-Dixon Line, the shortest line (which is often the most direct), the lines in the sidewalk, the police lineup, the out of bounds line, the finish line, the scrimmage line, the line you get out of when you are out of line, and the line you get onto when you are on-line.

"Shaded" lines go from thick to thin and create a subtle illusion of space. Thin areas recede while thicker sections advance.

Types of Lines

————————	Long / Short
————————	Thin / Thick
————————	Solid / Broken
————————	Straight / Curved
————————	Uniform / Irregular
————————	Neat / Sloppy
————————	Planned / Random
————————	Vertical / Horizontal

"*No one looks at the thing itself anymore. We look at what the thing does, at the traces it leaves behind.*"

— *Nick Samios*

Linear thinking (which is by far the most common type) identifies, sorts, arranges, and compiles information in a "straight line." Mathematics and logic are tools for developing skill at linear thinking. This is also called "vertical thinking." Horizontal thinking takes advantage of unexpected or illogical combinations of ideas. It is associated with intuition, creativity, risk-taking, and chance.

Some lines assist other activities. Notebooks have lines to assist handwriting; highways have lines to keep us in the correct lanes.

Some lines contain, as when we circle an area on a map, or when we string a line of floats to indicate a swimming area at a beach. Some lines separate, like the ropes hung to organize people at a bank or theater.

Some lines are symbolic, like the ones that make up the letters of these words. A child takes ownership of the world by drawing circles and lines and calling them people. In mathematics, a line indicates division, the act of cutting something into smaller pieces.

Linear

Linear (LIN e er)

1 Situations or compositions in which line
  is the dominant element, as compared,
  for instance, with plane, form, or surface

2 Things in a line or in an obvious sequence

3 A process that moves logically from
  point to point

linea (Latin) = line

> *Everything on earth is somehow related but rarely
> do we see it that way. We see and study it in bits
> and pieces; our world seems fleeting and
> fragmentary, and often, so do we.*

— *Philip Carlo Paratore*

Lines give emphasis, <u>like this</u>. They point to the most
important item on the list. They link labels to parts
on a drawing. They force connections.

Lines have history: a branch dragged through the
sand or the track of chalk arcing across a wall. Lines
are expressive, graffiti on a small scale.

Lines indicate inside and out, here and there, ours
and yours. Wars are fought over lines.

SEE:

Boundary	Edge
Center	Gesture
Confidence	Grid
Contour	Intersection
Dynamic	Perspective
Economy	Plane

Mass

1 A unified body of matter with no specific shape

2 The major part of something; majority

3 In science, the effect of gravity as registered on an object or particle

4 The total accumulation, as in a numberless crowd; the masses

maza (Greek) = barley cake, lump

Visually related to the bulk of an object—the accumulated sense conveyed by its external dimensions or surface. This often translates to the presence of a work, its ability to dominate the space it occupies. This sort of perceived mass is not measurable like physical mass but it is an important aspect of design.

Mass carries the idea of compactness and solidness. We are more likely to refer to a boulder than a bush in terms of its mass. Massive objects have stability and substance.

SEE:
Concrete
Form
Monumentality
Plane
Size
Weight

"Ugly things are ugly in much the same way, the world over."

– Bruno Munari

Module

1 A part of a construction used as a standard to which the rest is proportioned

2 A sub-unit that goes to make up a whole, generally through repetition of similar or identical units

3 A uniform structural component used repeatedly in a building

4 A self-contained unit that performs a specific task

modus (Latin) = measure

There is a modern feeling to this word; it is used to convey an industrial notion of repeatability and versatility. Furniture and housing are often modular.

The word module has overtones that go beyond its definition as a repeatable unit. Bricks are modules, for instance, and but they don't carry the implications of this word. It carries notions of more specific uses, and from that, the idea of universal or generic design. Where a brick is the beginning of creativity, as seen in its vast range of architecture, a module makes us think of a completed unit that allows for little creativity.

"What happens to the hole when the cheese is gone?"

— Bertolt Brecht

SEE:

Function
Grouping
Intersection
Pattern
Repetition
Structure

Monumentality

Monumentality (mon ye men TAL ite)

1 **Impressively large, sturdy and enduring**

2 **Of outstanding significance**

3 **Enormous and astounding**

4 **Larger than life size**

monere (Latin) = to remind, warn

Monumentality conveys the sense of being large, regardless of actual size. The Grand Canyon is monumental, but so is a grain silo, even though it is much smaller.

Monumentality is related to context, or the relationship of an element to its environment. It is also affected by simplicity, isolation and the quality of the surface. While a highly decorated surface may be seen as monumental (Notre Dame) it is less likely that this will happen in the absence of large size.

We instinctively respond to larger objects with deference. It is not a coincidence that temples, cathedrals, palaces, and courthouses are large. It is important to their function that they be imposing. But size alone does not make these buildings monumental. Attention to proportion, context, and surface all enhance the effect.

"*Standing in the middle of a quiet room in a quiet house while, like a curtain, the silent snow fell at every window. I heard all that quiet. It made noise.*"

— *Doris Grumbach*

SEE:

Anticipation
Center
Concrete
Mass
Plane

Motion

Motion (MO shen)

1 The action or process of change of
   position

2 A meaningful or expressive change in the
   position of the body

3 The way in which a body moves; gait

4 A prompting from within; an impulse or
   inclination

5 To signal or direct by making a gesture

movere (Latin) = to move, to gesture, as
                  in agreement

Real physical motion has direction, speed and duration. Visual motion is usually implied through shape, value, and lines. In composition these are used to lead a viewer through a piece, or back into the implied depth.

Our sense of physical motion is inherent—we don't need to be taught the difference between slow and fast. (We learn the words of course, but even before speech a child can distinguish between rates of motion.) Visual movement, however, is partially learned, as indicated by the way it relates to other learned activities such as reading. English-readers scan horizontally from left to right, even when looking at pictures. People who read in other ways, the Japanese, for example, use conventions of composition that are fundamentally different from those of the West.

Almost everything in the universe is in motion. Moving is vastly more common than standing still.

From its root as a gesture signifying agreement, we use this word to describe ideas formally brought before a group as a motion. The reason to act in a certain way, i.e. to move like that, is called a motive.

Every movement is both action and reaction as, in the human body, each movement involves a set of muscles, adductor and extensor. Without movement and return, action is frantic and misguided, tense and unrhythmical.

— Carla Needleman

Order

Order (OR dur)

1 A condition of logical or comprehensible arrangement among separate elements

2 A condition of methodical or prescribed arrangement to achieve proper appearance or function

3 Sequence; the customary procedure

4 Tidy, precise—an orderly arrangement

5 A command, as in the military. An orderly is one who takes orders, or one who relays orders.

ordo (Latin) = earlier

> *Confusion is a word we have invented for an order that is not yet understood.*
>
> – Henry Miller

Preposterous, which we know to mean "so inappropriate as to be beyond consideration," literally means "before and after," as in placing the proverbial cart before the horse. Incorrect order is preposterous.

Musical notes well-played might be pleasant, but they do not become a melody until there is an order in their arrangement.

We each have a need for order (a threshold of tolerance for disorder). One description of art is that it is humankind's attempt to impose order on the universe. This could be given as a definition of science as well.

We seek order. We will stare at a random collection of dots or puffy clouds in the sky until we are able to impose an order, to make it look like something.

Order is often a prerequisite to communication. Cat tree the up ran the....

Order implies a pre-existing structure. You can't put things in alphabetical order unless you know the alphabet. Things rarely fall into order by accident.

It is one thing to impose order and quite another to discover it.

SEE:

Balance	Integration
Center	Pattern
Control	Ratio
Craft	Rhythm
Grid	Stylization
Hierarchy	Template

Nature teaches the value of proper sequence. The seed, the sprout, the sapling, the tree. We refer to a correct (perhaps inevitable) string of events when we say "organic process."

The word organic is usually associated with rounded forms (snowdrifts, beach pebbles, plant forms) but because nature often works with geometric precision (such as crystals) the term is more accurate when describing a process.

Natural design is often the result of contradictory requirements. The arched cross section of an egg is rigid enough to withstand external force but will yield from the inside to the gentle tapping of a hatching chick. From this we get the sense of organic process as a creative solution through compromise. Also, organic thinking usually implies response to specific design requirements, as illustrated by the egg.

Organic

Organic (or GAN ik)

1 Related to growth in nature or representative of that process

2 Simple, basic, and close to nature

3 Having properties associated with living organisms

4 An integral part of something; fundamental; constitutional; structural

organikos (Greek) = instrument; a device to accomplish a task; organ

----

"Art need not be intended. It comes inevitably as the tree from the root, the branch from the trunk, the blossom from the twig. None of these forget the present in looking backward or forward. They are occupied fully with the fulfillment of their own existence."

– Robert Henri

SEE:

Abstract
Closure
Ergonomics
Gesture
Patterns
Stylization

Originality

1 **Pertaining to the beginning of something; initial; first**

2 **Freshness of aspect, design, or style**

3 **The power of independent thought or constructive imagination**

oriri (Latin) = to rise

The word origin refers to a starting point, the place from which something rises—a river or a thought, for instance. The word is given definition through its opposite, that which is derivative. The original is the thing that is copied.

One of the hardest tasks in design—or in life for that matter—is to deal with excessive freedom. In the absence of a limiting context, design becomes movement without direction, fickle and unproductive.

"*Don't worry about your originality. You could not get rid of it even if you wanted to. It will stick to you and show you up for better or worse in spite of all you or anyone else can do.*"

— *Robert Henri*

SEE:

Collaboration
Confidence
Eclectic
Sentiment
Stylization

Ornament is usually applied embellishment, generally not critical to the function or major attributes of the object. Firearms are frequently ornamented, but they would shoot just as well if the stock and barrel were plain. A Victorian house stripped of its gingerbread would still keep out the rain.

This is not to say that ornament does not function; rather, that its function is in addition to and often different from a primary function. The purpose of clothing is to cover and protect the body. The purpose of wedding clothing (with all its ornaments) is to distinguish an event as special. Through ornament we extend our involvement in a work, and mark it publicly as worthy of extra note. We ornament our churches more than our houses to distinguish their role as elevated from day-to-day existence.

In some cases ornament might be used to disguise the flaws of a mediocre design, which accounts for the suspicion it sometimes raises. But in other cases the form or structure exists largely as a base for the ornament, which brings complexity and visual density to the object.

Ornamental

mething that serves to decorate, embellish or adorn Something th

Ornamental (or na MEN tl)

1 Something that serves to decorate, embellish or adorn

ornare (Latin) = to adorn

"The purpose of good design is to ornament existence, not to substitute for it.

— George Nelson

A classic test to evaluate ornament is to remove it and observe the resulting form. A cathedral without ornament, for instance, is still wonderful because of its proportions, materials, and intervals. Ornament is added in this case to enhance rather than excuse a poor design. By contrast, a shopping mall devoid of its multicolored banners, benches, and marquees is often a boring collection of familiar forms.

es to decorate, embellish or adorn 1 Something that serves to decorate, embellish or ado

es to decorate, embellish or adorn 1 Something that serves to decorate, embellish or ado

es to decorate, embellish or adorn 1 Something that serves to decorate, embellish or ado

SEE:

Abstract	Monumentality
Decorative	Pattern
Eclectic	Sensuous
Function	Stylization
Harmony	Symbol
Integration	

Though parameters are often thought of as limitations, they can be springboards to better ideas. In the same way that a person's skill improves when playing against a challenging opponent, narrowly defined parameters can trigger unusual innovations. In poetry, complex meters and rhyme patterns are valued for this reason.

Design often starts by determining parameters, or by testing their flexibility. A mediocre designer might settle for the limitations as given, but a great designer pushes the limits of conventional thinking. Example: When the parameters of a chair are that it must be solid and have legs, the results are similar. When the parameters are extended, alternatives like the beanbag chair become possible.

The happiest people are not the people without problems. They are the people who know how to solve their problems.

– Robert Schuller

Parameters

Parameters (pa RAM e trs)

1 **Fixed limits or boundaries**

2 **Characteristic element**

3 **The outside dimensions, boundaries, particularly in reference to a task, a brief**

(Latin) para (alongside) + meter (measure) = outside edge

In design this term refers to the restrictions and challenges of a given project. It might include materials, size, cost, or many other factors, all of which will impact the decisions. Some parameters are visual (must be bright, must have a flat surface) and others are related to function (must have no sharp edges, must stand up to handling).

SEE:

Boundary   Form
Center   Function
Composition   Shape
Contour   Synesthesia

Patterns, or recurring activities and responses, are the very stuff of science. Without patterns of behavior, psychology and sociology would have no baseline against which to measure. We cut patterns for objects, we look for patterns of belief, and we pattern our lives after those people we most admire. Pattern is easy to understand and can be a Rosetta Stone in the way it crosses and links many disciplines.

There is no doubt about the importance of visual pattern, or that our ability to perceive pattern matures as we widen our experience of the world. A baby must learn to differentiate between near and far, then between hard and soft. It takes a while to discover the finer differences between shapes, colors, and textures that will become the building blocks of pattern. Geniuses, particularly in science and mathematics, are often credited with the ability to discern patterns that the rest of us miss. Pattern recognition is a large part of the business of being human.

"To divine the significance of pattern is the same as to understand beauty itself."

– Sôetsu Yanagi

Pattern (patrn)

1 An archetype; an ideal worthy of imitation

2 A plan, diagram or model to be followed when making things

3 A representative sample; specimen

4 To cover or ornament with a design

patronus (Latin) = patron, hence, something to be imitated, a model

When no pattern is obvious, one can be invented. Our ancient ancestors watched the passage of celestial events in a compulsive attempt to find order. In some cases, like the orderly revolution of the moon, they were able to find it. In others, such as the random patterns of stars, they invented a pattern by imposing figures of gods upon constellations.

What is map-making but a pattern that organizes a series of observations? The same may be said of etiquette (social patterns), of music (aural patterns) and of relationships (psychological patterns). Pattern gives us control—or the appearance of control.

Chaos theory tells us that there are patterns (or orders, or consistencies) in the world that escape our observation.

SEE:

Abstract	Module
Center	Progression
Control	Structure
Decorative	Symmetry
Figure/Ground	Template
Grouping	Texture

Plane

Plane (playn)

1 Any flat or level surface

2 A level of development, existence or achievement

3 In the visual arts, an imaginary flat surface that unifies or at least describes a series of points

planus (Latin) = flat

"Quality is not an act. It is a habit "

– Aristotle

Like "circle" and "center" this is a mathematical
invention, and can never really be achieved. It is
therefore an ideal abstraction, an unrealistic goal,
a dream.

A picture plane is the flat surface of a drawing, print,
or painting. In this instance the picture plane is real
but the illusion of space within that plane is false.

As in definition 3 above, "planar" does not necessarily refer to flat, though that is the common usage.
It is sometimes thought that an opposite of "planar"
is "organic", but crystals prove this incorrect.

SEE:

Abstract	Figure/Ground
Boundary	Mass
Center	Perspective
Concrete	Space
Contour	

In three-dimensional work, "positive" refers to the space that is materially occupied (the wood, stone, metal, etc.) as distinct from the areas of open space that are delineated by the positive areas. A hole in a donut is an example of a negative space.

The two-dimensional equivalent of negative/positive is figure/ground. If there is a parallel in music, we could say that the pauses are "negative". Just as a ladder depends on the spaces between the rungs to function, the pauses in music are essential to the nature of the work.

By understanding and manipulating the interaction of positive and negative areas, an artist is able to activate a composition, making it more interesting and unusual.

By extension, some time is programmed or controlled and may be thought of as "positive" time. The in-between times, the moments when we are waiting for something to happen, or adrift in a daydream, could be considered "negative" time.

Positive/Negative

Positive (POZ e tiv)

1 Moving in a direction of increase,
  progress or forward motion

2 Explicitly or openly expressed, irrefutable

ponere (Latin) = to place

Negative (NEG e tiv)

1 Indicating opposition or resistance

2 A thing or concept considered to be the
  counterpart of something positive

negare (Latin) = to negate

*"We shape clay into a pot,
But it is the emptiness inside
That holds whatever we want."*

– Lao-tzu (Tao Te Ching)

SEE:

Balance	Figure/Ground
Collaboration	Harmony
Composition	Hierarchy
Contrast	Tension
Dominance	

Progression

Progression (pro GRE shun)

1 Movement toward a goal; development

2 Steady improvement

3 A movement from one tone or chord to another; a succession of tones, chords, etc.

4 Course or lapse of time; passage

(Latin) pro (forward) + gradi (to step) = to walk forward

"The only road to authenticity lies through what has already been done. There is no deep art without deep historical awareness."

— Robert Hughes

Even though most visual art is stable, a sense of movement is created as a viewer experiences the work. The way a viewer's eye is led into and through a composition is part of the effect of a work. Like any journey, this can be fast or slow, interesting or boring, simple or complex. Some of the techniques used to direct this movement are rhythm, value, scale, and proximity. The effect, however it is achieved, is called progression.

In music there are progressions that "sound right." There is a story that when one of his musical friends came calling on Mozart and found him still in bed, the friend went to the piano and played one of these progressions of notes, leaving off the last one. Mozart, unable to tolerate the omission, jumped out of bed to strike the final note.

SEE:

Anticipation	Gesture
Composition	Interval
Continuity	Pattern
Dynamic	Repetition
Emphasis	Structure

Perspective

1 A mechanical system to represent three-dimensional objects and space relation-ships on a two-dimensional surface

2 The relationship of aspects of a subject to each other and to a whole

3 Subjective evaluation of relative significance; point of view

perspecius (Latin) = looking through

Early artists used overlapping to suggest space. The Romans and later artists had an intuitive sense of the basic rules of perspective (that parallel lines will appear to converge as they recede from the viewer) but it was not until 1417 that the Florentine architect Filippo Brunelleschi codified the laws of perspective.

Aerial perspective exploits the effect of the atmosphere on perception, as for instance when distant mountains appear lighter and less distinct.

"Results! Why, man, I have gotten a lot of results. I know several thousand things that don't work.

– Thomas Edison

Many people assume that proper use of perspective distinguishes "good art" because it makes a scene look "real." It's worth noting that perspective is an abstract system, like numbers or lines of latitude. All are relatively recent inventions of humankind, and all refer to a specific, some would say narrow, definition of reality.

We use the term to describe a specific impression, referring intuitively to the understanding that when we move around we change the view in front of us. Perspective also implies a larger, more comprehensive view, as in "Let's put this problem into perspective."

SEE:

Boundary	Grid
Center	Intersection
Composition	Line
Compression	Order
Contour	Plane
Control	Structure
Form	

Proximity

1 **Being near or next to; closeness**

2 **Referring to the closeness of elements**

proximus (Latin) = nearest

Proximity functions in design like the force between two magnets. When far enough apart they have no effect on each other, but when they come close together the pull is so strong they become one unit. In between there is a place where the tension of attraction is strong. A similar visual tension can exist between elements in a composition.

Proximity is dependent on the physical action of the eye and brain, and is probably influenced by our physical size. The speed with which the eyes can take in a composition will determine whether the elements are read as a unit or separately. Three dots scattered on a page have almost no relation to each other, but if they are placed close enough together (or if you stand far enough away) they will be perceived as a triangle. This effect is the result of proximity.

"Creativity requires the willingness and ability to declassify and restructure information and experience."

– Philip Calo Paratore

SEE:

Anticipation	Contour
Boundary	Figure/Ground
Center	Gestalt
Closure	Intersection
Collage	Line
Continuity	

Ratio

Ratio (RA she o)

1 Relation in degree between two similar things

reri (Latin) = to consider

Ratio means "same as." The most direct category of ratio is parallelism; the orientation of the second line is the same as the orientation of the first. Mathematically this would be expressed as a one-to-one ratio, written 1:1.

The second category of ratio is opposition, as illustrated for instance by lines that are perpendicular, or in opposition to each other. Another example is black and white, or up and down, which might be described as a ratio of 1:0, or something-to-nothing.

A ratio is a mathematical equivalent of an analogy —A is to B as C is to D. This is a ratio, and can be abbreviated like this: A : B : : C : D

In design the mathematics are less important than the sense of relationship, which is critical to a design—in fact, maybe the essence of design. It's not so much the parts, it's their arrangement that counts. The quantities and intervals of those arrangements are ratios. In the arts they are usually arrived at intuitively rather than by calculation, but they are no less important, even if they seem automatic.

SEE:

Abstract	Module
Contrast	Pattern
Dialogue	Progression
Harmony	Unity

"Without roots, they ain't no fruits."
— Willy Dixon

Resolution

Resolution (REZ e loo shun)

1 **Having determined to do something, to be resolute**

2 **The process of separating or reducing something into its constituent parts**

3 **An explanation, as of a problem or puzzle; a solution**

4 **In photography or magnification, acuity or sharpness; focus**

(Latin) re (again) + solvere (untie) = to completely untangle

The word is often used in art as an alternative to "finished," probably in the sense of definition 4 above, brought into focus. A composition is resolved when its elements are well chosen, well-placed and of a color and texture that best serves the needs of the work. Once it is resolved we can still ask if it is good.

A solution is an answer. Is this resolution a re-solution, a previously tried and therefore safe solution?

The word also describes confirmed opinions or intentions, as in New Year's resolutions.

SEE:

Anticipation	Formal
Balance	Harmony
Closure	Order
Composition	Structure
Control	Unity

"Every act of creation is first an act of destruction."
— *Pablo Picasso*

Repetition, which is related to rhythm, creates the opportunity for interval and rhythm. These in turn can create pattern, harmony, dissonance, and a sense of movement. Rhythm can be regular, progressive, alternating, or syncopated.

Rhythm requires multiplicity; one element cannot have rhythm.

Psychologists theorize that because our first experience of sound is dominated by the mother's heartbeat, all humans innately associate rhythm with security and well-being.

Rhythm is widely used in art, but predominantly in those branches of decorative arts that supply the sense of our day-to-day life—fabric design, wallpaper, architectural detail, and landscape. Remove from that list all examples of rhythm and you will have stripped the world of most of its ornament.

"The mysterious law of rhythm seems to be a universal law, since rhythm is coordinated movement, and movement is life, and life fills the universe."

— Henri Herz

Rhythm

1 Any kind of movement characterized
  by the regular recurrence of strong
  and weak elements

2 Nonrandom variation, especially
  uniform or regular variation in a process

3 The effect of recurring or repetitious
  lines, colors, forms, etc.

4 In music, the specific arrangements
  of accents and the relative duration
  of sounds

rhuthmos (Greek) = recurring motion
                   or measure

SEE:

Scale

1 A system of ordered marks at fixed intervals used as a reference

2 An instrument or device used in such measurement

3 A calibrated line, as on a map or architectural drawing

4 A progressive classification of size, amount, importance, or rank

5 Relative proportion, degree

scalae (Latin) = stairs

"*The artist recognizes existing relationships and arrests them.*"

– Louise Nevelson

We automatically make comparisons every time we receive sensory information. Objects are "too hot" or "safe to touch" because they are instantly compared to previous experience. This allows us to say "That's a big car" at a glance and be understood by people with a common experience.

In art, where the usual comparisons are less helpful, the artist or designer can provide a comparison and thereby create scale. We have a tendency to make size comparisons based on relationship to human scale. Return as an adult to a place known as a child and it seems so much smaller.

Scale can be used to direct a viewer through a site or image.

A "proper" sense of scale contributes to stability and comfort, while an "incorrect' scale makes us feel cramped or exposed.

SEE:

Contrast
Density
Gestalt
Monumentality
Ratio
Transition

Sensual

1 Pertaining to the senses or sense organs

2 Referring to the gratification of the senses and sexual appetites

sentire (Latin) = to perceive by senses, to feel

"Things good and generous take form in me, and the air is clear."

– Jelaluddin Rumi

Sensuous   can refer to any physical sense but
           usually applies to the intellectual or aes-
           thetic enjoyment of the arts, music, and
           nature

Sensual   is generally restricted to bodily sensations
           and to the satisfaction of physical
           appetites, particularly sexual

Artists and designers rely on the senses of viewers to
collect and sort the stimulation provided by their
work. The biology of the senses defines the boundaries of art. For instance we do not write music for
frequencies outside the human range, or paint pictures with infrared dyes. The arts are, by definition,
sensuous.

Most art also appeals to the mind, which has no
sense organs, but contains memories of the senses.

SEE:

Anticipation   Harmony
      Beauty   Organic
     Context   Sentiment
     Contour   Stylization

While there is an intellectual, rational aspect to art, it is commonly assumed that the primary arena of the arts is emotion. A successful painting or sculpture evokes emotional response, while often clarifying complex feelings. But, like sugar in coffee, too much of a good thing can become cloying. Greeting card illustrations are not considered in the same league as timeless works of art not because of a lack of technical skill, but because of sentimentality.

"Sentiment," referring to genuine emotion, clearly has an important place in art. By contrast, "sentimentality" is usually seen as a cheap substitute. John Gardner defines it as "the attempt to get some effect without providing due cause ... emotion achieved by cheating or exaggeration."

> " Good poems are not made of strong emotions, they are made of words."
>
> – W. H. Auden

Sentiment

Sentiment (SENT e ment)

1 Noble, tender or artistic feeling;
sensibility

2 An exaggerated emotional reaction;
a mawkish display

3 A thought or attitude based on
emotion rather than reason

sentire (Latin) = to feel

SEE:

Abstract   Context
Anthropomorphic   Decorative
Beauty   Integrity
Concrete   Symbol
Content   Synesthesia

"Shape" typically refers to a two-dimensional unit;
"form" is a parallel term for three-dimensional units.

Shape is the result of a line that travels back to its
beginning, an enclosed space.

Generally "shape" refers to a contour, the outer
reference of a form, usually a two-dimensional form.
Ask about the shape of a field and you'll learn it is
rectangular. Ask about the area and you'll be told it's
an acre. It's worth noting that descriptions of both
shape and area are necessary before you can understand the field.

*"Who can say what is a good shape or an ugly shape?
It comes back to function. It is a good shape for that
purpose, or it is ugly in that relationship. The contours
of a good shape will have meaning, emphasis, balance,
and rhythm."*

— Kenneth Bates

Shape

Shape (shayp)

1 The outline or characteristic surface configuration of a thing; a contour; form

2 Developed, definite or proper form

3 Something used to give or determine form, as a mold or pattern

schap (Old English) = to create, therefore to take shape, to impart form, or literally, "to cause to come into being"

SEE:

Abstract   Form
Boundary   Line
Compression   Organic
Contour   Plane
Figure/Ground

Size

Size (syz)

1 The physical dimensions, proportions,
  magnitude or extent of something

2 Considerable extent, amount or dimensions

3 To arrange, classify or distribute
  according to size

syse (Middle English) = fixed amount

Beyond the obvious measurable aspect of size, the term refers to relative measures—our automatic response to an element as "bigger than" or "smaller than" something else, usually whatever is closest.

Size is always relative. To prove it, answer this question: "Is this big enough?"

A 20 foot sculpture in an urban setting surrounded by skyscrapers will stand out at a glance because it is smaller than the architecture and larger than the people walking by. The same sculpture in a neighborhood of houses of similar height would have less visual power.

Experience has taught us that size is often related to time. Plants, animals, and people increase in size as they get older, up to a point. This intuitive link between size and time is unique among design elements. We do not assume that color, proportion, texture, etc. change as time passes.

"Beauty is not caused. It is."

   – Emily Dickinson

" To travel hopefully is better than to arrive."

– Sir James Jeans

SEE:

Space

Space (spayz)

1 **The intuitive three-dimensional field of everyday experience characterized by dimensions extending indefinitely in all directions**

2 **An interval or area between or within points or objects**

3 **An interval of time; period, while**

espace (Old French) = time interval

Because we are physical creatures, we have a built-in sense of space. We cannot imagine an existence without space. We are intuitively sensitive to tight spaces (fear of which is called claustrophobia), open spaces (agoraphobia), deep spaces (bathophobia), and crowded spaces (demophobia).

Space in a composition can allow entry and movement as the eyes "read" or travel through a work. If this space is cramped or vast, the experience of the work will be affected.

Spaces in both two-dimensional and three-dimensional work can become charged or loaded with heightened power because of form, scale, proportion and other factors. If two marks are set on a page with a small gap between them, the space between draws our attention more than other spaces on the same page.

Flat space has two dimensions—it is a mental construct that does not really exist.

Equal parts of figure and ground create an ambiguous space.

Structure

1 A complex entity

2 That which is constructed; a combination
   of related parts such as a building or machine

3 The position or arrangement of parts;
   constitution; make-up

structus (Latin) = built

> *I'm not trying to imitate nature,
> I'm trying to find the principles she's using.*
> —Buckminster Fuller

We commonly use the word for cases of a clear, perhaps mechanical arrangement; by inference, the result of an additive process.

Natural processes such as organic growth, crystallization, erosion, and sedimentation have been refining structural systems since the planet was formed. These offer valuable models for artists, architects, and craftspeople.

Sometimes structure dominates a form (the Eiffel Tower) and sometimes it is less obvious (a cloud).

In music and literature, the structure of a work is its underlying framework, the general outline of principle components.

If a surface or ornament is faulty it can be removed without affecting the structure. If the structure is at fault, no amount of superficial correction will set it right.

SEE:

Balance	Grid
Center	Hierarchy
Composition	Order
Context	Plane
Economy	Space
Function	Unity

"The problem with convention is that everyone's doing it."

Stylization refers to a nonspecific or generalized presentation. It can be achieved through

Exaggeration: Cartoonists often overstate physical features to create an image that does not read as a portrait of the person but as a symbol representing the person.

Simplification: An oval with wings on the side and a thin triangle of a beak at one end is understood to be a bird, though it lacks enough detail to tell the species. Most children's drawings are stylized in this way. As powers of observation and skill at representation improve, drawings become more detailed.

Communication depends on common ground—agreed symbols, usage, and definitions. Memorable communication requires a willingness to stretch these. Shakespeare invented many of the words he used and in the process improved the language.

A mannequin in a shop window is a stylized figure, accurate enough that we can understand the figure, but far from a portrait.

Stylized, Stylization

Stylize (STI l iz)

1 To make conform to a style or mode

2 To conventionalize

stilus (Latin) = writing instrument

SEE:

Abstract
Concrete
Content
Icon
Sentiment

Surrealism is an artistic style that uses peculiar juxtapositions to trigger unexpected or irrational associations. In this way it resembles dreaming, where impossible things happen as if they are normal.

Some surrealist artists compose through a conventional, rational process while others prefer to conjure up images through mind-altering activities like hypnosis, sleep deprivation, or drugs.

Surrealism asks fundamental questions about reality by suggesting that "real" means more than the physical world around us.

Surreal work may be weird, but not everything weird is surreal.

SEE:

Abstract   Eclectic
Anthropomorphic   Icon
Collage   Integrity
Content   Symbol
Control

Surreal

1 Derived from a literary and artistic movement launched in 1924 based on the liberation of the unconscious

2 An attempt to express the workings of the subconscious mind

(French) sur (beyond) + realisme (realism)

" Emotion is not something shameful, subordinate, second-rate; it is a supremely valid phase of humanity at its noblest and most mature."

– Joshua Loth Liebman

> "The role of art is not
> to give us pleasure,
> but rather to present us
> with something that we
> did not know before."

– Otto Baensch

SEE:

Symbol

1 **Something that represents something else by association, resemblance, or convention**

2 **A printed or written sign used to represent an operation, element, quantity, quality, or relation**

sumbolum (Greek) = put together. The word originally referred to a token that was broken in two so the parts could later be used to verify identity. A symbol, then, is a representation of authenticity.

Symbols are so common in our lives we cannot imagine being unable to understand their use.

An icon is a pictorial symbol; to know the object is to understand the symbol. A stylized picture of a hand will carry its meaning as a pictogram. Other symbols need to be learned: mathematical functions like + or - for instance. Some symbols are simple icons (cross, swastika, etc.), but symbols can be complex and dynamic. A symbol is defined by what it does, not what it is.

Symbols direct or confine a work of art to an audience. The iconography of Christian cathedrals, for instance, includes a complex collection of symbols that are more meaningful after instruction and memorization, like any other language.

Symmetry

1 An exact correspondence between the opposite halves of a figure, form, line or pattern

2 Beauty or harmony of form resulting from a symmetrical or nearly symmetrical arrangement of parts

3 Due or right proportion

syn (together) + metron (measure)
= measured together

" Beautiful things are valuable and useful precisely because they are beautiful."

– John Ruskin

SEE:

Kinds of Symmetry

Horizontal   Using an imaginary horizon or left-to-right line as the divider, top and bottom sections mirror each other. A landscape reflected in a still pond is an example of horizontal symmetry.

Vertical   This type uses a top-to-bottom line as a meridian, with identical images on either side of the line.

Radial   Through radiant, the word implies an outward direction. Radial lines are just as likely to draw attention inward, as for instance in a mandala.

Intuitive   Images that approach symmetry but are not exactly the same on the opposing parts. They "feel" symmetrical, but aren't. The human face is a good example.

Generally symmetry creates harmony, balance, and order, but risks being boring.

In reasoning we might speak of a symmetrical argument—a line of thought in which each point is matched by a similar, corresponding point.

SEE:
Pattern
Structure
Symmetry
Tension

"In kindergarten we drew three daffodils that had just been picked out of the yard; and while I was drawing, my sharpened yellow pencil and the cup of the yellow daffodils gave off whiffs just alike. That the pencil doing the drawing should give off the same smell as the flower it drew seemed part of the art lesson. Children, like animals, use all their senses to discover the world. Then artists come along and discover it the same way, all over again."

– Eudora Welty

Synesthesia

Synesthesia (sin es THEE zha)

1 **A phenomenon in which one type of stimulation evokes the sensation of another, as the hearing of a sound resulting in the visualization of a color; crossover between sensual perception**

2 **The use of terms from one domain to describe the effect of another, as in "hot colors" or "bright sound"**

(Greek) syn (together) + esthesia (to perceive, feel) = the ability to receive dual sense impressions

The use of cross-over descriptions not only makes for more interesting language, it can lead to untried solutions. When you have identified a shape as "quiet" you might more clearly create its opposite by imagining a "loud" shape.

SEE:

Anthropomorphic   Gestalt
Collaboration   Integration
Concrete   Originality
Content   Stylization
Contrast   Weight
Dialogue

Template

Template (TEM playt)

1 **A pattern or gauge used to convey a
correct shape. Often made of a durable
material, so in this sense it retains or
perpetuates a shape**

templum (Latin) = small piece of wood

A template conveys information about size, shape, and location, and in this way can span time and distance. An African tilemaker could relocate to another continent with his grandmother's template and continue to make work that would appear identical to hers. In this way a template is a bridge across time and space.

A template often contains important information that is not otherwise easily available. The template might be more valuable than the finished piece— the goose rather than the golden egg.

In computer software a template is a generic version upon which a customized program can be built.

"One never uses the rules, one only feels them."

– John Ruskin

Tension

Tension (TEN shun)

1 The condition of being stretched tight

2 Mental strain; intense nervous anxiety

3 A force tending to produce elongation or extension

4 Strained relations between persons; uneasy suspense

tensio (Latin) = making taut, stretching

A man learns to skate by staggering about making a fool of himself; indeed, he progresses in all things by making a fool of himself. "

– George Bernard Shaw

Perhaps because of our learned experience of having a tense object snap, we view tension with a sense of foreboding. In plot development, tension is used to sustain interest. Tension can be both a visual and a psychological phenomenon; it gets our attention.

Physical tension is the result of pulling in opposite directions. Visual tension can result from disparity in media and content, symbol and message, or pattern and form. An example of the latter is camouflage, in which tension between real forms and painted shapes create so much visual ambiguity that the eye prefers to "not see" the object.

Tension describes situations or structures in flux; unresolved, about to happen. It is important not to confuse tension with agitation or chaos. Tension is present in the quiet before the storm. Tension results from a dynamic opposition of formal elements, and suggests unresolved relationships.

SEE:

Compression
Composition
Content
Dynamic
Fragment
Intersection
Proximity

Three categories of texture:

1 Literal texture that is the result of the surface of a material or object. We know the texture of the skin of an orange by feeling it. We generally use the term to indicate rough texture.

2 Remembered or implied texture such as when we see a photo of an orange. We don't physically experience the texture by touching the photograph, but we nevertheless distinguish the surface of the orange as being different from the table on which it sits.

3 We also use the term conceptually to refer to a complex or vague pattern, particularly when considered abstractly or from a distance. We might refer to the texture of an argument, or piece of music.

"His writing had the texture of whipped cream. And unfortunately, about as much meaning."

— Bill Smith

Texture

Texture (TEKST shur)

1 The appearance of a fabric resulting from its woven arrangement of fibers

2 A grainy, fibrous, woven, or dimensional quality as opposed to a uniformly flat, smooth aspect; surface interest

3 The representation of the structure of a surface as distinct from color or form

textus (Latin) = woven thing

Sometimes it is texture, not music, that soothes the raging beast within us. Imagine sliding into a bed made with crisp freshly-laundered sheets, or lying back on the pleasantly prickly grass of a hillside bathed in sun....

Textures are often charged with emotion. Most people have a positive response to soft and fuzzy; that's why we pet cats and wear soft fabrics around our neck.

People avoid certain foods not because of their taste but because of their texture.

SEE:

Contrast
Density
Dominance
Figure/Ground
Integration
Structure
Unity

Time

Time (tym)

1 A nonspacial continuum in which events
   occur in apparently irreversible succession
   from the past through the present to the
   future

2 An interval separating two points on this
   continuum, measured essentially by selecting a regularly recurring event, such as
   sunrise, and counting the number of its
   occurrences during the interval

3 A suitable or opportune moment or season

4 In music, the beat; the pace of the rhythm

tima (Old English) = time

"   *How sour sweet music is*
When time is broke, and no proportion kept!
So is it in the music of men's lives."

    – *William Shakespeare*

Time is the fourth dimension—just as every object must have a measurable height and width and depth, so everything can only exist in time. To say it another way, as physical beings we cannot imagine the absence of space or the absence of time.

A visual artist must be aware of "viewing time," the time needed to perceive a work. In performance or cinematography this is in the control of the artist, for instance, in the running time of a film. As long as the viewer doesn't get up and leave the theater, the director can control how much time elapses between one event and another.

In the traditional formats of the visual arts (painting, sculpture, etc.) the shape and direction of elements and the nature of the composition will render a work easy to take in at a glance or a visual maze that requires time to decipher. An example of the former is a portrait, which is perceived at a glance; an example of a "slower" composition is a cityscape.

SEE:

Anticipation
Closure
Compression
Continuity
Rhythm
Surreal
Transition

Transformation

Transform (tranz FORM)

1 To clearly alter the form or appearance of a thing

2 To change the nature, function, or condtion; to convert

(Latin) trans (from one to another) + formare (form) = to change form

In one sense, this is the primary description of what an artist does—canvas and pigments become a portrait; a lump of clay becomes a cup. Intangible ideas are translated into tangible objects. Transformation is our middle name.

Some transformations are one-way—once the clay becomes a pot or sculpture we don't tend to see it as a lump of clay. In some compositions the parts dissemble; the work is dynamic and seems to coalesce into an image, then dissolve away. This makes the viewer part of the transformation process.

Transformation isn't difficult—throw a brick through a window.

"The only thing constant is change."

—*Traditional saying*

SEE:

Anticipation
Closure
Continuity
Invention
Join
Order
Progression

Transition

Transition (tran ZI shun)

1 **The process of changing from one form, state, activity, or place to another**

2 **Passage from one subject to another**

3 **(music) A passage connecting two themes**

(Latin) trans (across, over, through) + situs (location, place) = to move from

Transitions happen as we view any object. Artists and designers manipulate them to give the work direction, pace, and structure.

Surveyors use a sighting device called a transit to establish a base line for taking measurements.

Transition occurs along lines of movement and in a direction, as in "horizontal, slow, left-to-right" or "radial, two-dimensional and rapid."

"*Life is essentially playful. Of course, it plays a bit rough at times.*"

—*Tom Robbins*

SEE:

Anticipation	Interval
Closure	Motion
Continuity	Progression
Contrast	Rhythm
Dialogue	Tension
Hierarchy	

Unity

Unity (YOO ni te)

1 The state of being one; singleness

2 The state, quality or condition of accord or agreement; concord

3 The combination or arrangement of parts into a whole

4 The ability of a composition to coordinate its various parts into a stable whole

unus (Latin) = one

The task of artists is to organize elements into a comprehensible whole by simplifying, organizing and unifying.

– Kenneth Bates

Unity is the effect of the whole exerting a greater force than would be expected from a simple collection of the parts. When you taste the ingredients in food, that's analysis. When you sit back and savor, that's unity.

Unity defies formulation but will often include careful attention to hierarchy, rhythm, and balance.

Unity is the positive effect of establishing a sympathetic relationship between parts. The more diverse the parts, the greater the challenge —and the reward. We deal with issues of unity when we select the clothes we wear or when we decorate our homes—"Do these go together?"

Connect the dots—repeat every mark, pattern or color—the effect will be consistent but this is not unity, any more than playing the same note over and over could be called a melody.

Thin strands can become a strong rope because of the way they are assembled. Diverse parts can create a powerful composition when organized to create unity. Note that even a disjointed composition can achieve unity, as we see, for example, in a Pollock painting or a crowded street. The lack of order provides a pattern of its own, which unifies the scene.

SEE:

Balance
Composition
Figure/Ground
Gestalt
Grouping
Order
Resolution

When we see a black and white photograph, we are seeing the world rendered exclusively as value, as the colors without the hues.

Value can be used to organize a composition: by placing areas of changing value strategicall, a viewer's eye is guided into and around a picture plane. The degrees of contrast and relative amounts of value will give movement and speed to the work. Because distant objects appear lighter in nature, value creates the illusion of depth.

- In painting and drawing, value is usually created with media (black paint; gray paint)

- In graphics such as typography, value is usually created by density (tightly grouped, loosely grouped)

- In three-dimensional work value is usually the result of hollows or cavities that create shadows, or "hold onto the light"

Value

1 The relative lightness or darkness of color in a picture

2 That aspect of color by which a sample appears to reflect more or less of the incident color

3 Lightness or darkness; the amount of white or black

valere (Latin) = to be strong

Colors, textures, materials, surfaces and content all make it difficult to evaluate the role of value in a work in progress. A black and white photograph can be a useful device to filter out these other elements.

"The pattern satisfies me, and what more do I want?"

— *Robert Henri*

SEE:

Volume

Volume (VOL yoom)

1 The size or extent of a three-dimensional
  object or region of space

2 Broadly, the capacity of such a region or
  of a specified container

3 A large amount

volumen (Latin) = a roll of parchment, "to
                  contain a vast amount"

"The pleasure of a thing well done is to have done it."

    – Traditional saying

This word traditionally refers to an interior space, particularly a space that is contained. A bowl has volume, as do a lake, a coffee cup and a cathedral. This is a first cousin to mass; both words refer to the overall size of a form, but mass is generally concerned with outside dimensions, while volume refers to a measure of the interior.

In some situations, volume is an important parameter of design, for instance in a 32-ounce bottle. In other cases volume is important but less specific, as in a vase.

Where an internal space is visible, volume presents an opportunity to create interest by contradicting a viewer's expectation.

A second use refers to sound, "turn up the volume" or, literally, how many sonic waves are pushed into the air around us. When we like the music, we turn up the volume.

SEE:

Compression   Ratio
Contour   Shape
Mass   Space
Monumentality   Structure
Parameters

Weight

Weight (wayt)

1 A measure of the heaviness or mass of an object

2 The gravitational force exerted by the earth or another celestial body on an object

3 Influence, importance, authority

wighte (Middle English) = to lift, hence to take the heft of, to measure

"The artist's aim is to turn his audience into accomplices."

– Arthur Koestler